Rememberings

Sinéad O'Connor

Rememberings

PENGUIN BOOKS

PENGUIN BOOKS

UK | USA | Canada | Ireland | Australia
India | New Zealand | South Africa

Penguin Books is part of the Penguin Random House group of companies
whose addresses can be found at global.penguinrandomhouse.com.

First published in the United States of America by Houghton Mifflin Harcourt 2021
First published in Great Britain by Sandycove 2021
Published in Penguin Books 2022
001

Printed and bound in Great Britain by Clays Ltd, Elcograf S.p.A.

The authorized representative in the EEA is Penguin Random House Ireland,
Morrison Chambers, 32 Nassau Street, Dublin D02 YH68

A CIP catalogue record for this book is available from the British Library

ISBN: 978-1-844-88542-8

www.greenpenguin.co.uk

Penguin Random House is committed to a
sustainable future for our business, our readers
and our planet. This book is made from Forest
Stewardship Council® certified paper.

Dedicated with love to all staff and patients
at St. Patrick's University Hospital, Dublin

to my father, John O'Connor,
and to David Rosenthal, Bob Dylan, and Jeff Rosen

Contents

Part Three

Foreword

I CAN'T REMEMBER any more than I have given my publisher. Except for that which is private or that I wish to forget. The totality indeed of what I do not recall would fill ten thousand libraries, so it's probably just as well I don't remember.

Chiefly I don't remember because I wasn't really present until about six months ago. And as I write this, I'm fifty-four years of age. There are many reasons I wasn't present. You can glean them here. Or most of them.

I was actually present before my first album came out. And then I went somewhere else inside myself. And I began to smoke weed. I never finally stopped until mid-2020. So, yeah, I ain't been quite here, and it's hard to recollect what you weren't present at.

Making music is hard to write about. I was present then. In the place deep inside myself that only I know. But if you could talk about music you wouldn't need music, so perhaps the things I talk about here are not always music. But they are the sum of what I can recollect and tell from my youth until now.

I have left some people out because I know they prefer privacy and others because I want them to be pissed when they look for their names in the book and don't find them.

That I wasn't present explains why there are two very distinctly different voices in this book, one leading up to the tearing of the pope's picture in 1992 and a new one afterward. This is because it took me four years to write anything after "the pope chapters" (the night before and the night of *SNL*), years during which I lived in and out of mental-health institutions sorting out my reasons for not being present. Afterward, a new voice began speaking. And I hope this is acceptable to the reader. (It's pretty much the best I can do.)

I see the first voice as a ghost's and the next as a living woman's. Both are equally important. There was a symbolic death and rebirth. And you can hear it. I am, in fact, rather proud of it.

Now, I ain't gonna be winning the Booker Prize anytime soon. And I ain't Bob Dylan or Shakespeare or even in the class of my amazing brother Joseph as a writer. But I've told my story as I remember it and tried to tell it the way I speak. I imagined a certain person I was talking to as I was writing or talking the chapters. Never gonna tell you who that was, though.

I was very young when my career kicked off. I never had or took the time to "find myself." But I think you'll see in this book a girl who *does* find herself, not by success in the music industry but by taking the opportunity to sensibly and truly lose her marbles. The thing being that after losing them, one finds them and plays the game better.

I am an older woman now with a different voice. So this is only my first memoir. My intention is to live a long life and keep diaries this time so I won't forget. However, it was necessary for me to let the child inside me speak because she needed to speak. And because I did, she is older now and chooses to remain about seventeen.

Please know that I have deep and infinite love and compassion for both my parents, who did their very best in what was a very difficult time for Ireland and for Irish people. And my father remains my idol, having borne more pain than any human being I know and having borne it so heroically. We are a family made of soldier DNA. There are military great- and great-great-uncles. And this has stood to both my father and myself.

I especially hope that by letting the child speak I do not cause offense or upset to anyone in my family. I haven't discussed anyone's experiences but my own. And I apologize in advance if anything I've written does cause upset. It was not my intention.

My intention was to put all the pieces of the jigsaw that was me out on the floor and see if I could put it together. To be understood was my desire. Along with that was my desire not to have the ignorant tell my story when I'm gone. Which was what would have happened had I not told it myself.

If I hope for anything as an artist, it's that I inspire certain people to be who they really are. My audiences seem to be people who have been given a hard time for being who they are. It ain't easy being green —maybe they don't know they are the reason I get to be who I really am. Onstage, I can always be who I really am.

Offstage, not so much. I never made sense to anyone, even myself, unless I was singing.

But I hope this book makes sense.

If not, maybe try singing it and see if that helps.

PART ONE

Prologue

HEY, HEY, WE'RE THE MONKEES!

BEFORE WE BEGIN, for the purposes of clarity, here is the architecture of my family and when I was with whom.

My mother, Marie, and father, John, married in 1960 and set up home in Crumlin, Dublin, where they had been raised. Three years later my brother Joe was born and they moved to middle-class Glenageary, far away on the other side of town. Then in 1965 came my sister, Éimear. Then me fourteen months later, in 1966. Then in 1968, my brother John.

In 1975, my father sensibly left my mother for reasons this book will help you glean. He was given custody of us and we went to live with him and his new love, my (lovely) stepmother, Viola. But me and my little brother stayed only maybe six months because we missed our mother.

At that point I was nine. I stayed with my mother until I was thirteen and then I went, by choice, back to live with my father. I was unable to adjust after what had been going on in my mother's house, so toward the end of my thirteenth year, I went to what is politely called a "rehabilitation center for girls with behavioral problems." (I think the whole world knows a refund is owed my father for that, as it clearly didn't work.)

At fifteen I left the center and went to a boarding school in Waterford. I joined a band that summer, and when I went back to school, I missed the band. So in December, after I turned sixteen, I ran away from

3

the school and got myself a studio apartment, a bedsit, much to the horror of my poor father. He eventually agreed to let me stay once I agreed to remove the nose piercing I'd also gotten. He paid my rent but none of my bills, so I had to get jobs. He's a genius.

My father's second wife, Viola, has three daughters from a different marriage. So I have three stepsisters. Viola and my father also have one son, Eoin. So he's my brother also.

In 1985 my mother died in a car crash. I was eighteen. Later that year, after being invited by Ensign Records to sign a contract with them, I left for London.

My first child was born when I was twenty, three weeks before my first album was released. I have three other children and, so far, two grandchildren.

Sinéad, at about age five
COURTESY OF THE AUTHOR

THE PIANO

IT'S CHRISTMAS AND WE'RE at my paternal grandma's house, the one that usually smells of cabbage (the house, not her).

The lights around the tree mean the other downstairs lights are off. The grown-ups are in blue shadow with their backs to the parlor, concerned with one another, running all up and down the stairs. I'm little enough that they won't notice me if they don't look any lower than straight ahead. My grandma's parlor is verboten for me without adult supervision. The Christmas tree is in here. I got away with sneaking in to feel the presents, but something else is what I really want.

Against the wall rests an old piano. The keys are yellow, like my granddad's teeth. There are echoes in the notes, a strange sound, like the ghost bells of a sunken ship. I sneak in here often by myself because the piano summons me. It makes the air around itself vibrate in huge waves with just the slightest suggestions of colors so as to catch my attention.

When I play the notes, it sounds so sad. The thing is desolate. Once, at dusk, I asked it why. It answered, *Because I'm haunted,* and told me to put my ear against its underbelly, the flat panel of wood that's in front of your shins when you're playing. I pressed my right cheek against it, and the piano said, *Now play some notes.* I played, stretching my left arm up so my face would stay where it was. Underneath the notes above, I heard a lot of voices jumbled together, all whispering over one another. I couldn't make out what they were saying, there were so many of them.

I shot up and said, "Who are they?" The piano answered, *History*. It said, *They're stuck. They can't get out if no one plays me and I can't breathe with them all in here*. It said, *I don't mind if you play me badly, I just need to be touched. Play me very softly, gently, gently, only barely, because I am a very tender thing, and the ghosts are very sore*.

I said, "You still didn't tell me whose voices they are." It said it didn't want to tell me. I asked it why. It said, *Because of war*. It said, *A child shouldn't know about war*. It said, *People don't talk, so their feelings fly into musical things*. It said, *The ghosts are things people don't want to remember*.

In my parents' house on Christmas Eve we knelt before the crib in the hall to place the Baby Jesus in the manger, because he can't be there before midnight, and we sang all the songs that make me cry.

My father had to help me off my knees and up the stairs to bed. I couldn't walk right because the Christmas songs were in my body. They bent and twisted me so I couldn't stand straight. My father understands about songs making me cry. He doesn't think it's weird. I'm always worried it means I'm weird, that songs make me cry and be crippled and I'm only a child. He sings me "Scarlet Ribbons" when I'm all tucked in. His voice sounds very sad. He feels sad a lot. Like me.

Lovely ribbons, scarlet ribbons
Scarlet ribbons for her hair

I'm mind-blown by the song. That there are such things as angels, and that angels left ribbons, and that children's prayers get answered, and that the *capo di tutti capi* can outrank parents.

But it isn't ribbons I want, I want songs to take me away to that other world. I don't like reality. I don't wanna find myself back in it after three minutes and have to hang around in it until the next chance comes to have it vanish.

MY GRANDFATHERS

MY FATHER'S FATHER is a cabinetmaker. He keeps canaries and homing pigeons in a wooden-and-wire-mesh birdhouse he made that runs along the bottom of his garden. I really like him. He's plumpish compared to my mother's father, and he's a giggler, a smoky laugh he has.

I used to wrap my whole hand around his index finger and drag him to the birdhouse so I could see him make the pigeons fly off with messages in little barrels tied to their feet and then fly back to him empty-footed. Once he asked me would I like a fat bird to send a message for me, so I got him to write *Hello, God, from Scamp.*

When I asked him, my granddad said Scamp is my nickname because a scamp is a rascal, a bold thing, and I'm the boldest of all my mother's children. But he threw his head back and cackled smokily after he said it. Looked like a big child himself, his eyes got so happy. He likes me for being bold. Maybe he was the boldest of his mother's children.

In the evenings, he and my grandma go out on their own together for a glass of porter because they're in love. I like seeing them going down the road when I'm swinging on their gate in the summer. They met on the same street, which was Francis Street, in the Liberties, an inner-city part of Dublin, historically a working-class neighborhood and home to Guinness and other breweries. But when my father was twelve, his people had to move out of the Liberties to Crumlin, a more residential neighborhood near the city center. That's how come my father's parents live on the same street as my mother's parents, which is Keeper Road, so my parents met on the same street they grew up on, just like my father's parents did.

My mother's father is a bread-delivery man and wears an old-style black waistcoat with a pocket watch and a long black coat and black pants. He is very long and skinny, so all in all he looks like de Valera on a diet.

His and my granny's house is like most of the houses of old people. There are worn-out pictures of popes all over the wall and above the fireplace, along with Padre Pio and Mary and Jesus. Halfway up the narrow stairs, there's a glowing red Sacred Heart lamp on the wall. It's really scary; no one wants to go up there when the other lights are off.

My mother's dad doesn't like women who wear makeup. Says they're "Jezebels." His insults are usually biblical. "Judas!" he'll shout when so-and-so's name is mentioned. Or "Creeping Jesus!" The only thing he wants in life is quiet but he can't say *quiet* properly because he's from Westmeath. He roars, "Quite! Quite!" at us over the top of his newspaper when we're being too noisy, which makes us giggle, so he has to roar it again.

To make up for tormenting him, I stand behind his chair and rock him real softly in the evenings when it's just me and him so he can fall asleep. I make music in my head to the rhythm of the chair so that I keep my movements gentle and don't wake him. It goes *One-two, three, one-two, three, one-two, three*, over and over.

...and my granny's house a long time ago the picture
...some worn-out pictures of ... was all over the railroad
...along with Padre Pio and ... Virgin Mary and John

Kitty O'Grady, Sinéad's maternal grandmother

AUGUST 1977

ELVIS IS DEAD. I'm crying so fucking much I can't make my bed. My body won't work. I keep trying to throw the sheet across the bed but I can't, my arms won't work. I try crawling across the bed with a corner in each hand but I can't, my legs won't work. I'm in trouble with my mother because I haven't got the bed made. I'm too embarrassed to explain why I'm dripping snot and tears all over the clean sheets or why I keep falling on my knees and standing up again. I think she likes Elvis too. Figure she secretly knows why I'm a mess. She doesn't get very cross about the bed. She doesn't get cross at all, actually, which is most unusual.

I need a new father now that Elvis is gone. My father isn't dead, I just ain't seen him for a very long time, because my mother doesn't like him. Fact, they pretty much can't stand each other. It's scary when they're together. It's not much scary on our own with our dad, though. But she's different.

I don't go looking for any father because I have God. And God sends me stuff because I talk to Him. Naturally He's the number-one father. But I'm a kid. I need a father's voice, and poor God don't have a voice. I like voices for some reason. I dunno why. Sometimes people's voices make me want to cuddle them. But I'm really scared of cuddling.

My body won't work if someone tries to cuddle me. I like my aunt

Lily and it hurts her feelings I won't cuddle her. I really want to. But I freeze and in my head I see a mountain of wolves all covered in blood, so much that they can't move, and only one wolf is running about, the one who was at the very bottom of the pile when whatever happened happened and it has no blood on it. It's looking for help.

I ain't seen my granny, my mom's mother, for a while either. She has a gentle nice voice. She likes me. She says I'm honest and never to say sorry if I don't mean it. She lets me have everything I'm not supposed to have to eat. She can make me fall asleep by just gazing in my eyes when I'm tucked up in her bed. I like her clock's ticktocking. Makes me hear music. Ain't seen her since I was maybe six. She came all the way from Keeper Road on all the buses with my birthday present. My mother wouldn't let her in. My granny cried and stood at the door looking at me sitting on the stairs. I was big-eyed scared. She begged my mother. She wanted to see me. She had on her tan coat. She gave the present to my mother. My mother said I could open it on the stairs and then Granny would have to leave, but she still couldn't come in the door out of the December cold. My granny likes my birthday because it's a holy day as well and she loves God as much as she loves me.

It was white pajamas with tigers all over them. I loved them. I made my eyes smile at my granny because I knew I wasn't allowed to let my face smile. She did the same. But her face was tear-strewn. And like I said, I ain't seen her since. I started smoking properly because she does and I like the smell of her. I pray a lot, like she told me. I love God, like she told me. I only ever ask for Him to be with me.

I come downstairs one morning, after Elvis, and hear a kind man's voice singing to a girl that she needn't cry anymore. I go to the record player. I make my brother Joe play it again. I say, "Who's he?" "Bob Dylan." I see from the album cover he's as beautiful as if God blew a breath from Lebanon and it became a man.

I'm not allowed to touch the record when my brother isn't home. I wait at the window every day because he has a summer job. I run out into the street and around the corner to watch for him. I never know when he's coming home. Things aren't safe at all when he's out. My mother doesn't like little girls.

I like this Dylan man's singing. In my head I call him Lebanon Man. He has an empty baby carrier hanging open across his chest. I slip myself in. His voice is like a blanket. He's really tender and he loves girls. I have his chest to fall asleep on.

So I've stopped knocking on doors around Glenageary asking people if I can be their child. Been doing that on and off since I was about six. They always only bring me home anyway, imagining my mother to be like other people's mothers. Dylan'd never be deceived. Though some of them did give me cheese balls and such. One family was having a Tupperware party when I knocked. The nice lady let me in because I was crying. She said she couldn't keep me but I could stay for a while. So I chose to sit under the table because there were so many people. She gave me loads of food. I would have liked to stay with her. When she brought me home, my mother acted all nice at the door. Bob is a way better dad than Elvis anyway. That's what I thought about all the time her knee went into my stomach up against the wall.

Sinéad in her communion dress
COURTESY OF THE AUTHOR

LOURDES

WE JUST GOT back from Lourdes five days ago. Bit dramatic. Let's just say an "episode" was had by my mother, after which a priest was cajoled by me and dragged by the arm to come and help her on account of that's the whole reason we went there.

Well, it's the reason I went there; the others had to come because the trip was my requested confirmation present. Deal being, Jesus's mother might see about helping mine. I didn't tell anyone I was thinking in such a way. They just put it down to my being obsessed with the whole Lourdes thing because I've been reading about it for years. My granny told me about it because of my birthday and because my second name, Bernadette, is the same as the nineteenth-century maiden who saw the Virgin Mary there.

On the day before we were to leave Lourdes and return to Dublin, no cure had been found for my mother's madness, so I decided to go priest-catching at about four p.m. My chosen victim was dragged by his sleeves in protest (mine) at his not being as eager as I was for him to go to work, ambling as he was along the basilica gates in the sunshine with his newspaper. He relented at length because I was too much for him (I did the big eyes), had him gawggling at me like it was insane to believe miracles could happen in Lourdes even though that's the whole deal his bosses employed him to sell.

I'd told my mother I was going for ice cream, so as I shoveled him up the road with one hand on his back and one still on his sleeve so he couldn't escape, I told him the bullshit story he was now to sell to my mother regarding how he met me, hoping he'd sell it better than he seemed capable of selling the Lourdes story.

So up he goes to her room. I sit in the little hotel lobby watching the pretty French ladies trying really hard not to look pretty because they're in Lourdes.

He comes down after a while with his newspaper under his arm, his cowboy-looking black hat on his head, his green eyes watery-looking and fixed to the floor. As he brushes past my chair he signals with his head that I'm to follow him out. "There's nothing I can do for her," he says and tells me I'm to pray until I'm eighteen and can leave home, unless I'm able to leave any sooner.

I'm thinking, *Oh, great. A hopeless priest. How the fuck did he get stationed here?*

See, I had a Lourdes miracle of my own some years back. I had a verruca, a wart. On the left foot beside the little toe. Big painful thing with a black center. It was like the girl who loves Anachie Gordon in the old folk song—its heart would not remove.

So I was booked to go into hospital to have the verruca surgically removed, a thing of great glory, for it meant I'd be spoiled rotten for at least two days and have a ton of sympathy and everyone having to be exceedingly nice to me, not to mention I'd have a fair few days off school, and there would be ice cream and jelly for certain at the hospital.

The night before I was to go in, my mother took me into the bathroom and put some Lourdes holy water my granny had given her years back on my verruca. In the morning, the verruca was gone. Utterly and completely vanished. No one would have guessed it had ever been there; there wasn't a trace of it. So I know Lourdes miracles do happen, unlike my priest friend.

We had gone to Lourdes via a travel agent. Picked up at the airport by a tour bus. We drove with about twenty other people who were on our tour. We didn't do just Lourdes; we first went to a town called Nevers to see the convent where Saint Bernadette lived and died after her visitations from Our Lady.

They had her tiny body in a Snow White glass case on display, and people filed in there every day to see it, a grotesque tableau. It reminded me of the Dublin zoo. They had a crocodile in a glass enclosure the exact length and width of its body, so it couldn't move, with enough water to almost cover it while leaving its back exposed. At the top of the glass there was a gap with the ceiling. The grown-ups would throw coins through the gap so they'd land on the crocodile's back to see if they could annoy it because it couldn't move. I wonder what the zoo people did with all the coins.

Bernadette's body was dug up three times in the first thirty years after her death, in 1879, so people could take parts of her bones for altars. An altar isn't sacred, apparently, if it doesn't contain some part of the body of the dead. Sounds more devilish than God-ish to me.

On the tour bus we had a guide called J. He worked for our local travel agency back home and he was very kind to me. He sat up front and had a microphone for telling people what they'd see if they looked left or right out the window. He started loads of sing-alongs, though, and my mother nominated me a bunch of times to sing "Scarborough Fair," which I duly did, with much feeling, because I had secretly fallen in love with J. I was sad when we all got back home, because I missed seeing him every day.

I'd been pining and singing the song all alone. Today I got sick of doing that and decided to walk the two or so miles down to the travel agency to declare my love and ask him to marry me.

It was lunchtime when I got there but J. was sitting at his desk, talking on the phone. My heart began pounding with fear. It had never occurred to me he might have a wife. Maybe he was talking to her. He finished his call and saw me in the doorway. He beckoned with his hand for me to come in, looking surprised that a child had made her way alone to arrange some possible trip through a travel agent.

I said I needed to speak with him in private. J. brought me into a small kitchen, sat me at the little round table, poured me a glass of milk, and asked if I wanted some biscuits, but I couldn't eat because I was so sick with love.

Not having the courage to speak and having prepared for this eventuality beforehand, I produced a written declaration. He read it, smiling the whole time, as sunlight shone through the open window onto his lovely brown stubble. When he finished reading, he folded my letter carefully and asked me if he could keep it. He said it was the loveliest thing he'd ever read but that he was way too old to marry me or even be my boyfriend because he was thirty, but that one day I would meet a boy of my own age and that would be better.

He also said he was the kind of man who loved other men. I'd never heard of such a thing before, so he had to explain a little. He said sometimes God just makes men who fall in love with men, or women who fall in love with women. He asked would I mind keeping what he'd told me to myself because he said people didn't really agree with men loving men. He said people didn't often recognize what God loved, and he said they sometimes didn't love what God loved.

J. told me I was never to believe any kind of love was wrong if it was true love and to always be brave enough to tell someone I loved them, because it was brave of me to have told him, and it had made him feel very happy. He said that if a grown-up ever behaved like a boyfriend with a child then that was wrong, so I was not to be telling grown men I loved them after today because not all grown-up men were as safe as him.

When he asked me why I loved him I said it was because he was gentle. So he said I'm to always make sure anyone I love is gentle. Then he said I could come and see him anytime I liked for milk and biscuits and he was gonna be my friend.

So I wasn't upset because I made him smile and because he was so nice to me. I walked home very proud I'd been so brave and already imagining what my future boyfriend might be like. There's a boy called Gary who lives near me who keeps asking me to go to the roller disco with him. I haven't asked my mother because she is very strict, but maybe I will.

MY AUNT FRANCES

SHE'S SIXTEEN AND I'm six. She has Down syndrome. She lives all week in a care home on the Navan Road with the nuns because my granny and grandfather are too old to look after her properly. But she comes home every weekend and I love her. She is like a big walking heart; she loves everything and everyone. She hasn't any badness in her, only good. She's very dainty and ladylike. She has tiny hands like her sister—my mother—and she's the only person my mother adores.

I'm often at my granny's when Frances comes home for the weekend. Frances takes my granddad's yellow suitcase-looking record player and drags me upstairs to her room and locks us in. She has a stack of records, all by the Irish pop singers Danny Doyle and Luke Kelly. Frances is in love with Danny Doyle. She'll say to me, "Isn't he lovely? Isn't he lovely?" in that funny way she has of talking through her nose. I have to agree he's lovely or she'll swat me softly across my head. But he isn't lovely at all. He has a beard and he looks like he drinks too much beer.

She puts the record player on the bed and every time she plays an album she makes me hold the cover and read out loud every word of what is written on the sleeve and labels, back and front, inside and out. If I can't say a word, she helps me, pacing about the room like a school-teacher. She makes me feel every millimeter of the record's packaging too, with my fingers and palms and even the sides of my face. If I don't do it slowly and touch every millimeter, she swats me.

She has lots of baby dolls, which she loves. She makes them dresses. My mother helps her because my mother was a dressmaker before she got married, but in Ireland you can't work anymore if you're a married woman.

Frances's favorite doll is called Brenda. But me and my sister accidentally broke Brenda and Frances hasn't forgiven us. Every time she sees us she says, "Youse broke Brenda." I understand how she feels because my cousin bit the beak off my favorite cuddly toy, which is a penguin called Charlie that my father got me when he was away working somewhere. I don't like my cousin now and I'm never going to speak to him again. Frances is a lot nicer than me.

Primary school in Dublin
COURTESY OF THE AUTHOR

THE TRAIN

I WENT BACK to school this week after three months off. And then I pretended to faint a bunch of times at my desk so the nuns would send me home again. They're so worried about me after what happened that I got away with mere Golden Globes–worthy performances; they didn't have to be Oscar-winning.

Sweet! If I so much as blinked too much, seems like they would have sent me home. Usually I'm the bad girl, because I'm always stealing people's lunches (particularly peanut butter sandwiches) or shoplifting from the dress shop or stealing money for the candy store from the teachers' handbags in the staff room.

Sister Clothilde brings me to the chapel regularly to pray that the urge to steal will leave me. So far it hasn't worked. But that's because my mother likes me to steal.

Mrs. Sheils, who was a teacher, used to ask me if my mother made me do it but I said no. She'd ask me where the welts on my legs came from or about the massively swollen black eye I once had.

She'd say, "It's your mother, isn't it?" But I'd deny it.

If my mother found out I'd told, she'd murder me. I felt bad lying to Mrs. Sheils because she's lovely. I don't know why she likes me, but she does. I'd like to be her girl. I'd like to be going home with her every afternoon. She'd look like she was about to cry whenever I said it wasn't

27

my mother. Her face would go all red and she'd reach deep into her handbag and give me money for sweets and pat my face all gentle like my granny does.

I'm jealous when I see the other girls walking down Merrion Avenue after school with their mothers' arms around them. That's because I'm the kid crying in fear on the last day of term before the summer holidays. I have to pretend I lost my field hockey stick, because I know my mother will hit me with it all summer if I bring it home. But she'll just use the carpet-sweeper pole instead. She'll make me take off all my clothes and lie on the floor and open my legs and arms and let her hit me with the sweeping brush in my private parts. She makes me say, "I am nothing," over and over and if I don't, she won't stop stomping on me. She says she wants to burst my womb. She makes me beg her for "mercy." I won the prize in kindergarten for being able to curl up into the smallest ball, but my teacher never knew why I could do it so well.

I love Jesus because He appeared in my head one night when my mother had me on the kitchen floor. I was naked and had cereal and powdered coffee all over me. My mother was saying all this scary stuff, and I was curled up so she could kick me on my bottom. Suddenly, there Jesus was in my mind, on a little stony hill, on His cross.

I never asked Him to come; He just arrived. He had on a long white robe and blood was flowing from His heart all the way down His robe and down the hill and onto the ground and then onto the kitchen floor and into my heart. He said He would give me back any blood my mother took and that His blood would make my heart strong. So I just focused on Him. When my mother was finished with me, I lay on the floor until I knew she had closed her bedroom door. Then I tidied up all the stuff she'd thrown about and set the table for breakfast.

Once the Holy Spirit came and sat with me too, though I didn't ask it to. It happened this way:

There was a button missing off my dress, which used to be my sister's dress. And we were supposed to go away for the weekend to my mother's friend's house. I got beaten up naked again and my mother took the light bulb from my room and locked me in and went away with the others. When I'm frightened, I find bits of paper and write, because I'm not allowed to say I'm angry at my mother. So I write and then tear the pages into tiny little pieces and eat them so she won't find them.

This was on a Friday. When it got dark, I felt about my room until I found some paper and a pencil. I wrote to God. I said, *Please help me.* I was kneeling on the floor, facing my bed. Then, out of the corner of my eye, I saw a small, white, very misty cloud come sit to my left, a little behind me, and it stayed there all night.

But the Spirit didn't come back on any of the other days.

I didn't eat anything all weekend and I peed on the floor. When my mother got back, she was cross and hit me for that. I had to go to hospital later that day because I had a horrible pain in my stomach. The nice young doctor said, "This child hasn't eaten." My mother said I'd eaten goulash, but I hadn't.

She locked me in and went away another time before this, but in the night my daddy came and broke the door down and took me to the doctor. I don't know how he knew I was there. He was upset when he saw all the dried blood on my face. We didn't say much in the car.

She locked me under the stairs a lot too.

When I'm at home, I can hear Mrs. Sheils's voice in my head, calling my name.

I hear Sister Clothilde too, just calling my name. I don't know if she likes me. I suppose she slightly does. She's just not a smiley person —she's the headmistress, so I guess she isn't allowed to smile. It must be so depressing being a nun. I'm really scared God will make me want to be one. I regularly pray that He won't, although I've felt some calling to work for Him because He is so good to me.

The last time I heard Clothilde talking in my head at home, I'd been sent to bed during the daytime for saying Princess Anne was "preggers." I was really angry about getting sent to bed. Next thing I knew, there was Clothilde's voice and, as I happened to look at my closed bedroom door, the handle went fully down and the door opened but no one was there. I went to the sitting room to ask my mother if she had opened the door. She said she hadn't been upstairs, so I don't know who opened the door. Maybe it really was Clothilde.

Not long after this, I was standing in Blackrock Station with my sister after school waiting for our train to Glenageary. A train passed through at full speed and a blond boy of about fourteen, in a gray school uniform, opened a door on the racing train and it grazed me on the right side of my head.

I was bleeding so much that my gray school gabardine was soaked from shoulder to knee but my sister and I just got on our own train when it came, got off at our stop, then walked up the long hill home, about a mile. My mother was cross that I hadn't kept my ticket so she could sue the train people. The doctor came and put stitches in my head while I lay on the couch. I had very long hair. My hair was caked with blood by the time he was finished, but he said I wasn't to wash it for a month for some reason. So it got very smelly. He also said I was to sleep in my mother's room, and she was to watch me in case I went unconscious. I had a nice time with her then. She made me a bed on the floor. And during the day when the others were at school, she taught me how to blanket-stitch and made me banana milkshakes.

That's why when I got back to school, I put on the fainting act. So she'd keep me home and love me.

LOST IN THE MUSIC

I ASKED MY mother's doctor to put her in the hospital because of what happened after my brother Joe ran away. She called the police, and they put out an APB, and he agreed to meet her near our house. She took me in the car with her. Joe got in and told her he wasn't ever coming home. She told him if he didn't she would put me in the passenger seat of the car and drive into oncoming traffic in order to hurt me and force him to come back. He didn't believe her. And he got out of the car and walked away.

Then she did it. Put me in the passenger seat and deliberately smashed into a car that was coming the other way. Luckily we were both okay. But I did scream at her.

When we got home I called her doctor. And he came and said that for our sakes, he would put her in the hospital.

My siblings and I are banned from visiting my mother at the hospital. I'm glad because it means I don't have to tell her I've been fired from my job at the café. They found out I stole fifty-four pence, but they knew I'd been stealing money all along. I can't stop stealing. I got fired from the clothes shop for stealing skirts and cardigans for my mother. We all get summer and Easter jobs. Mostly at restaurants. We lie about our age.

We've been alone in the house for almost the entire summer now without a soul checking on us since they took her to the hospital—not even the doctor, nobody. We're having the time of our fucking little lives.

I want to be a ballet dancer. I love ballet so much. I do nothing but draw pictures of feet in pink or red pointe shoes. I dance in pointe shoes but I got into them too early; my teacher would be worried. It's really bad for your feet but I love it so much I can't stop. I'm too shy to dance in front of people, but on my own I can do anything I want. My shoes are pink with satin ribbons and I love them more than anything on earth. Me and my sister went to the Rotunda Hospital to ask for plaster of Paris to make a cast of the slippers, but the doctor told us people only have babies in the Rotunda so they didn't have any.

I love Margot Fonteyn so much. She's so beautiful. I draw the Firebird with colored pencils. I love Rudolf Nureyev. And when the two of them dance together, it's like they're one bird and it's a dove.

My mother gave me a big book about Margot Fonteyn for Christmas once. I go over the photos in pencil with tracing paper, then draw them on real paper and color them in with markers.

But my ballet teacher said I can't have any more lessons until I get my back fixed. She said there are people who can fix it. It's been hunched and crooked all my life. I can't straighten my spine. She says it's worse since the train accident. She gave me a letter for my mother.

When ballet music plays, the whole universe goes spinning around me like a circle of those whirling dervish men I saw on television. Only they're whirling so fast I can't see them. All I can tell is that there are planets and space and some pinks and greens and light and dark blues and reds and sparkles. But they're the kind of colors you can see through, they're so misty.

As I wrote as a kid:

There's someone in the music too, it's not a person
Its hands reach out for mine, it isn't human

It's dark blue and green and made of space
It wants to put its arms around my waist
It wants to dance with me and whirl me by
It seems to know me but I don't know why

I love disco music too, Sister Sledge and all that stuff. I've heard lots of songs on the radio in the car and we always watch *Top of the Pops*. I love "54-46 Was My Number." I love the reggae song "Israelites" too, and "Uptown Top Ranking." I never heard any reggae except those three songs and I love them.

I wish I knew what *strictly roots* from "Uptown Top Ranking" means.

I heard the Impressions too; they have a song called "Fool for You," about a man who loves a woman who is mean to him. It's clever because they made the music sound like a fool flopping about the place.

I also love David Bowie. I saw him as part of Marc Bolan's show. I don't know what to think of Marc Bolan because he seems like he is pretending to be someone, but David Bowie isn't pretending. He's not boring or square and singing like teachers tell everyone to sing. He has his own voice. Marc Bolan has someone else's voice. I think he doesn't like himself because he wouldn't need someone else's voice if he liked his own.

I saw another reggae man called Bob Marley on the telly. He had on a blue shirt and he had really long hair all in sections. I was up really late. He was singing about stirring something up but I didn't know what he meant.

My brother Joe played me some music on Ireland's Radio Nova, "Stairway to Heaven" and "Freebird." I love them, especially "Freebird." I don't understand "Stairway to Heaven" because the singer says the lady buys the stairway but you can't.

Joe and I have been on the roof of the garage rocking out to "Freebird" and a song about husky dogs pissing in yellow snow. We pretend we're a band. When the others aren't around, I get up there by myself and rock out to "Honky Tonk Women." I just shake my long hair about all over my face, like headbangers do.

I love the Sex Pistols. I love "Anarchy in the UK." And "Pretty Vacant" and "God Save the Queen." And I love the Boomtown Rats and Stiff Little Fingers. All the screaming, I love that.

In real life you aren't allowed to say you're angry but in music you can say anything. I love all the noisy electric guitars. My brother played me a Bob Dylan song called "Idiot Wind." It's really angry and he says loads of mean things to someone. It's really brave. He isn't pretending to be nice all the time.

I found an old broken transistor radio in the garage a while back. I think it might be my grandfather's. I'm not sure but it's really old. I took it all apart and put it back together and it works! I don't even know how I did it. I sneak it under my pillow and listen real quietly at night. I like the song about sunshine on a cloudy day and the one about tears of a clown and the one called "Just My Imagination." I like the Supremes as well. And Ray Charles. And Elvis Costello and Dire Straits.

My mother always has on Ireland's national RTÉ radio. It's really boring and depressing. They never play happy music or talk about anything happy. It's all really sad songs like the one about the art teacher who tells a boy that flowers have to always be red or the one called "Tears on the Telephone." They play the show bands too. Show bands are so horrible. They're Irish but they play terrible covers of country and western songs, and they wear horrible shiny outfits and do really stupid dance songs like the one by the Shadows.

But mostly on RTÉ, it's talk all day. Boring, stupid, sad, or square stuff. Lots of stuff about the war up north too, on the news. I'm really scared when I hear about bombs and fire and old people bleeding and everyone screaming and tanks and soldiers and people throwing things and even little kids watching in the streets.

And that horrible Ian Paisley man in the priest suit screaming with his eyes all bulging. I'm sure he is the devil because my mother says the devil always dresses as a priest. I can't move when I see him on TV. I don't like it when he comes on and my father isn't there. Years ago, when I was little, I had to get my father because I was watching Laurel and Hardy, and Laurel went down the drain in the bath and I was really upset. I wish it could have been the Paisley man instead.

RTÉ television plays the national anthem every night before closing down and we're all supposed to stand.

There's a really miserable show on the radio, a lady named Frankie with a really deep croaky voice who reads letters from people who have bad boyfriends. Bad boyfriends are ones that don't ask their girlfriends to marry them or who want to have sex with them before they marry them. She also reads letters from men who are too shy to ask their girlfriends to marry them. And letters with stories of broken hearts and deaths or tragic losses.

The station plays that miserable Marianne Faithfull song constantly too, the one where she sings "someday I'll get over you." My poor mother bought the record. If I ever hear it again, I'll lose my mind. She may get over my dad but I'll never get over being subjected to such a terrible song.

Same goes for Marianne's cover of Shel Silverstein's song "The Ballad of Lucy Jordan," about a woman going mad.

I have a new job now. In a nightclub. Because my mother's boyfriend told me a nightclub is a place where people go to dance to disco music and not the boring Irish dancing music that squares listen to. I'm thirteen but I made myself up in loads of heavy foundation, blusher, mascara, and lipstick. Walked in and told the manager I was sixteen and he believed me!

So far, this is the greatest job of my life. I mean, I get to wear a white blouse with a nice black skirt. I stole the two of them from Dunnes, the big department-store chain.

My job is to give out the pink dinner tickets. The men aren't allowed to drink as soon as they come in; they have to order some dinner. So they first queue up for a numbered ticket from me, then they queue for the food. Usually it's some disgusting curry, not at all like my mother's curry, which is the best thing you could ever eat. I love it because my face burns for ages after. I always chop the onions when she's making it because onions don't make me cry.

The men are nice and I like how the place gets smoky and everyone is a little bit drunk. I like the disco lights, how they bounce around the room off the huge disco ball that hangs from the ceiling in the middle of the dance floor. I like how the smoke and the pillars on the dance floor make it so you can't really see anyone properly.

I turn up for work an hour and a half before the place opens because the DJ said I could. He is always there early too, before me. He has to practice his set, so while he is doing that at full volume, he puts on the disco lights for me and the smoke machine and I change into my ballet shoes and my shiny blue stretchy disco pants that my mother would kill me for wearing because they're so tight. I stole them too.

I have the floor to myself for a good half an hour with only me and the DJ there and I make him promise not to look. He's nice to me. He doesn't look. I know because I keep my eye on him. He ducks down behind his mixing desk and gets busy with his lists.

WILL YOU STILL LOVE ME
TOMORROW?

OKAY, I DID a bad thing. But I didn't know it was bad, so it isn't a sin. That's what the Bible says, anyway. If I were to do it again now that I know it's a sin, it would be a sin. As long as I never do it again, I'm grand.

I was sitting in Pizzaland with my friend, showing her a funny finger-pointy trick my father taught me years ago. A waiter thought I was calling him over. I wasn't. But it became apparent he thought I was flirting with him. And he started flirting away with me. This was rather flattering because he was American and, consequently, gorgeous. Bleached-blond semi-dreadlocked hair and the cool accent. I'm only fourteen but when he asked me what age I was, I said, "Eighteen." I had on a ton of makeup, so he believed me.

American men are cool; they're never squares. Irish men are total squares. There's nothing sexy about them. Me and my sister used to talk to all the Mormon men in town just because they were American, even though our mother told us not to. They looked so handsome, like movie stars in their suits. They worked in pairs, standing in the streets trying to convert Irish people (so sweet they thought such a thing could ever succeed). But all they were converting were teenage girls from lusting after teenage boys to lusting after grown men, particularly grown men in suits.

Me and my sister told two of the Mormons we wanted to go to their house to talk about the Bible. It was only partly a lie because I do like to talk about the Bible. They made us popcorn, and sitting there with their jackets off and white shirts revealed, they told us all about how being a Mormon is different to being a Catholic. I can't remember one word they actually said. I was fantasizing myself gloriously happily married to one of them, living on a farm with nothing to do at the end of the day's work but talk about the Scriptures and get naked and slide all over him in his suit.

Anyway, this poor waiter—Paul was his name—flirted away with me, thinking I was eighteen. I never had sex before so when he asked me to go to his flat in Smithfield with him, it never struck me it was sex he had in mind. Genuinely. I thought we'd kiss and stuff, like people my age do, but not have sex.

Once we'd been kissing for a while, though, it became apparent that the "whole enchilada" was required. I thought, *Well, I have to lose the virginity at some point.* Most of my friends have done it. I wasn't cool at all because I hadn't, and this was my big chance. I climbed into the bed with him, excited even though I was also really nervous, delighted my deflorist was to be an American. Nervous because I hadn't a clue what you were supposed to do. I'd only ever had one sex-education lesson in my life. A plump old nun stomped into our classroom one afternoon —we'd never seen her before, we had not the slightest idea why she was there. She picked up the chalk without uttering a word and in one stroke drew a giant erect penis pointing toward the ceiling. It must have been about a foot tall, with a massive pair of balls underneath.

Before she'd finished drawing, we were on the floor laughing. Literally clutching ourselves so we wouldn't piss. By the time she swiveled round to begin whatever speech she'd had in mind, she was already scuppered; she'd lost control of the room. We couldn't get up. It never struck her to erase the penis. Instead, she stood in front of it pleading for order over and over, to no avail. Eventually she ran out of the room. That was the end of sex ed.

I've looked at my stepmother's book called *The Joy of Sex*. It's kind of horrible because there are drawings in black pencil of the man and woman. The two of them are really ugly. He has a horrible beard. They put me off the whole idea of sex, so I hadn't actually read the book. I haven't learned a thing.

There's a drawing in the book that's made me really scared. It's in a chapter on things a woman has to know how to do. It's illustrating the fact that you'll get dumped if you don't do them perfectly. The man is in the bed, angrily pointing at the door, while the woman is ashamedly gathering her clothes to get dressed and leave. He's saying, *Get out and never darken my bedroom door again*.

So I'm in the bed with this American, Paul, thinking, *Oh God, what do I do?* But I didn't really get time to worry long. As soon as he attempted to get inside me, he realized I'd never had sex before because he couldn't get in at first. Eventually I bled.

Afterward, he figured out I wasn't eighteen. When I admitted I was fourteen, he nearly had a heart attack. Made me get dressed straightaway, then walked me in the dark to get a bus home, all the while imploring me never to lie about my age again because apparently it's illegal to have sex with someone if they aren't eighteen and he could get into trouble with the police.

On the bus I wondered if I looked different. Would the passengers say to themselves, *There's a girl who isn't a virgin anymore*, and consequently think me cool?

MY MOTHER'S
RECORD COLLECTION

MY MOTHER LOVES music more than anything apart from cooking and, in particular, baking. She went to the Cordon Bleu cooking school in town. She makes amazing cakes with ornate decorations. She takes us to a weird old lady's house to buy dolls for the top of them. I think the lady is so old, she must be dead, but all the sugar in her body keeps her walking around. Her house is dusty and doily'd.

We use the big dining table in the sitting room only when it's Easter or Christmas and the lovely cakes are on display. But the rest of the year my mother's record collection is spread across the whole width of it, like a deck of cards.

She has John Lennon, Johnny Cash's prison albums, Waylon Jennings, Ella Fitzgerald and Louis Armstrong's *Porgy and Bess*, and Simon and Garfunkel's *Bridge Over Troubled Water* and *Sounds of Silence*. She has Woodstock, Van Morrison's *Moondance*, the Velvet Underground, Lou Reed, lots of Beatles records, and *The Jungle Book* soundtrack. She has lots of Elvis records too; the first album I ever bought was an Elvis double album called *Le Roi du Rock 'n' Roll*. (I also love Elvis movies.)

My mother has lots of Frank Sinatra but there's something about him I don't like. She also has a guy called Donovan and Otis Redding. Then there's an old guy with a huge nose, Jimmy Durante. He sings a song about the lost chord; I love that song, it's funny.

She has Nick Drake, Dusty Springfield, Joni Mitchell, Cat Stevens, Stevie Wonder, Mike Oldfield, and a weird Rick Wakeman record called *The Six Wives of Henry VIII*. She also has a ton of records by the famed operatic Irish tenor John McCormack. She says when she hears him singing, she feels like she's died and gone to heaven. I feel like I'm living in hell every time he opens his mouth.

My favorite singer in all her collection is Barbra Streisand. I love to watch her movies. I love *Hello, Dolly* and *Funny Girl*. She's so beautiful; her nails are so long and she wears cool eyeliner. I love her speaking voice and her singing voice. She doesn't sing like anyone I've ever heard—her voice is way more free, kind of like David Bowie but different, obviously. Both of them sound like wild birds. Everyone else sounds tame. I would love to sing in musicals one day and be like Barbra. I would also like to grow my nails, but I bite them until they bleed. My mother has very long nails. She's always putting that disgusting-tasting stuff on mine so I won't bite them, but it gets on my sandwiches.

I love John Lennon too. I feel like he's my brother. He's been singing in my sitting room for as long as I can remember. His voice sounds like an angel's. He's bold as well, like me. And he's angry, like me. I like his angry voice. He's sad, too, and he's brave about saying so. I liked it when he stayed in bed. I wish I could do that. I like his wife; she's cute like a little kitten and I love kittens. I think it must have been her idea for them to stay in bed because she loves him, she wanted to cuddle him all day. I wish I could cuddle the two of them. I wonder if they would like a little girl.

WHY I SING

THE SERGEANT CAN see I want to puke. But he isn't gonna let me leave. I wanna run up the road to Harvey Proctor, a really ancient man who keeps pigs. Sometimes I wander down to him because he lets me pet the babies. I can't remember how I met him. He's very nice to me. The mother pigs are very smelly, and so are the big fat fathers; they just lie about in stinking muck all day. I wish I were a pig. I love the babies and their little squeaky oinks. I really wanna bring one home but Harvey says I can't because it would grow too big to come out of the house.

I got caught because I drew a big cross-eyed toothy face on the toilet door in a pub in Dalkey last week with a blue laundry marker and then I went back a few days ago with my collection tin and the owner started chasing me. He said he knew I was stealing from the collection tins and he'd called the police. I ran in the toilet and climbed out a tiny window. I'd been at home really scared ever since, and I decided I better come to see the sergeant and tell him what's been going on because if my mother finds out I got caught by the police, I'm gonna need police protection.

My mother herself is addicted to stealing. Has been for as long as I can remember. When the collection plate is passed around at Mass, she takes money out of it rather than putting money in. When the new traffic circle was made at Avondale Road, she drove down in the night with trowels and black rubbish bags to steal the just-planted baby bushes.

When they planted new bushes, down she went again and took those. I don't know what she did with them. When she was in hospital she took the crucifix off the wall. She even sent me home with the weighing scales from her hospital room under my school gabardine. She goes to visit houses that are for sale just so she can steal trinkets. She has a gazillion books all piled about three feet high on the floor all around her bedroom. She stole every one of them. She steals everything.

I'm addicted to stealing too. That's why I like to sing hymns. It isn't bearable to be such a bad person. I have to do one holy thing so I can live with myself.

I knock on people's doors and sell them their own flowers I've stolen from their gardens. I stole a ton of money for weeks from all the pockets in the changing rooms at the yacht club; I got caught because I asked a milkman in a van to give me bills for my coins and he got suspicious. I stole a wallet from a handbag in the staff room at the shoe shop when the lady let me in to try on ballet shoes. I went back to see if I could do it again, and they kept me there and called the police, but the policeman was really nice to me. I begged him not to tell my mother and he didn't.

About a year ago, I started first-aid lessons. The people who run the course said they were having a Flag Day collection. You get a tin and badges and you go around to people's houses and ask for money and then the money gets used for good things. They said there was gonna be a prize for whoever collected the most money by the following Sunday and the prize was a silver Cross writing pen. I really wanted to win it because posh pens remind me of my father. I walked all the way home from Blackrock to Glenageary knocking on doors and my tin was almost half full when I got home. I was real excited to tell my mother I did a nice thing and I might win the pen.

We have a rough red sofa with some faded gold design. My mother took the cushions off, got a knife from the kitchen drawer, and removed the lid of the tin. There was strong aluminum foil underneath. She flicked the knife around the circled edge and removed the foil. Then she gave me back the tin and told me to empty the money onto the sofa.

We piled the coins into fifty-, ten-, five-, two-, one-, and half-pence pieces. She took all the silver coins and said I should keep the copper coins.

I was horrified. But I went along with it because she was happy with me. She was glad I got money. I saw that if I kept getting money, things would be safe.

Outside the big bank in town, the charities set up trailers and invite people to collect money on their behalf. They give you a tin and a roll of badges and when they ask who you are, you just make up any old name and address. They don't even check. Mom and I have been getting all kinds of tins from all kinds of charities. We haven't left any of them untouched. We have posh accents so everyone trusts us. We've been at it since the day I came home with the first-aid tin. We've been driving around all the pubs in Dublin in the nighttime collecting money. Hundreds of pounds on the weekends, sometimes so much we empty a tin out in the car and then drive on to the next place. On the weeknights it's about half as much.

Mom's sitting here now giving an almost-but-not-quite-Oscar-worthy performance for the sergeant. Making out like she doesn't know anything about the tins and she's outraged. That's why I want to puke, but the sergeant won't let me leave. He wants me to watch her sell me down the river. She doesn't know he's promised he won't lock me up because I've told him the truth. She doesn't care if I get locked up. The sergeant looks like he wants to punch her.

I don't think I love her anymore.

There's a big house full of priests up the road from my school. I knocked on the door one morning instead of going to class. A lady just a bit older than my mother opened the door and I said I wanted to see a priest by myself. She brought me into a big sunny sitting room with a short dark wooden wavy-shaped table. She went away and came back carrying a tea tray with flowery china cups and saucers and a plate of Madeira cake. She said the priest would come soon and I was to be polite and eat. I thought about the confirmation choir songs while I waited because they started singing in my head. I don't even like them except for one. It says maybe God can change you into something good when you're something bad.

He was a gentle nice priest, with dark hair. He wasn't very old and he had a calm voice. We talked for ages. I told him I was a thief and God could see me. And that I was a terrible person, which I am. I told him everything I told the sergeant today. And I told him how I had stuck my wooden stilts in the fire at home and tried to walk across the carpet with them in flames.

He listened really carefully and after a while he asked me what job did I think I might like when I'm an adult. I told him I liked singing.

He said, "Ah! Did you know that he who sings prays twice?"

I said, "I didn't know, Father, but I think it must work for girls too because I can sing my mother to sleep with 'Don't Cry for Me Argentina.'"

He said, "And don't you remember a thief died beside Christ and was rewarded with paradise because he was penitent?" He asked me what girl singers I liked. I told him I loved Randy Crawford. He made me promise him that when I get a job, I will give back all the money I took; he said then I would be square with God. He said I could go busking if I didn't want to wait, but I don't know how to play guitar. I just carry my brother's guitar case empty around Blackrock so everyone will think I'm cool.

But I'm going to keep my promise.

THE HOUSE OF THE RISING SUN, PART ONE

I'M STARING AT the reflection of my eyes in the window of the back seat of my father's car. I'm thinking it will always be the same two eyes looking at me all my life. I made him stop at the record shop so I could buy a copy of Bob Dylan's *Desire*. I left my mother's house months ago, a little while after we got caught over the charity tins. I've been at my father's house since.

His house is kind of chaotic. It's like there's three families: my father's, my stepmother's, and the one they made together. My stepmother has three daughters. The oldest is the same age as my sister, the next is the same age as me, and the next is the same age as my little brother but my little brother isn't here, he's still at my mother's. Then my father and stepmother have a son who is nearly five. There are only four well-behaved people: my sister, my five-year-old half brother, my youngest stepsister, and my stepmother. The rest of us, including my father, are completely out of order.

I like Viola, my stepmother. She is very slim. She's from the north of Ireland with a soft accent and a soft voice and always a huge toothy smile. She has short blond hair and she can speak fluent French. She likes calligraphy and teaches me some. Very rarely, she will have one glass of sherry and have to be helped to bed. She's so innocent. She

47

adores the ground my father walks on. I dearly wish she were my mother. Sometimes I'm angry at her because she isn't. I was cross with her for not meeting my father earlier.

My mother said we're not allowed to like my stepmother. When we'd go driving through town, she'd point out shops where she said my step-mother buys clothes and say, "Only hooers go there." She'd point out hotels and clubs, too, and say the same. It made me and my sister laugh and want to go to all those places. She said, "Only hooers pierce their ears," so I got my ears pierced a few days after I left her. Got my hair cut real short too because "only hooers" do that.

Viola loves God like I do. We talk about God a lot. She's very gentle and she's really in love with my father. I don't know how she puts up with him. He's a little trigger-happy. Maybe it works because she's so über-gentle. She couldn't lose her temper if she tried. When she gets cross with me and my stepsister, we laugh at her.

My siblings and I lived in my father's house for nine months or so when I was nearly nine. As I mentioned, I used to steal everything, sweets and such from the shops, and I was generally a pain in the ass, arguing all the time as to why I didn't have to do a thing Viola told me. Poor woman, having me and my big mouth dumped on her.

She'd take my hand and, thinking she was acting really angry, she'd slap my fingers but so lightly I couldn't feel a thing. With each slap she'd pronounce a syllable of the following sentence in her northern Irish accent: "Don't dictate to me 'cause I won't have it," trying as hard as she could to grit her teeth but not being able to because she didn't have any badness in her.

The reason my siblings and I lived with her then was that my mother lost custody of us because the day my father left her, she put us to stay in a hut he'd built us in the garden. Once he'd gone, we started crying. She said if we loved him so much, we could go live in the hut. I knelt on the ground in front of the gable wall and wailed up to the landing window to get her to let us into the house when it got dark. She never responded and off went the light in her bedroom and everything went black. That is when I officially lost my mind and also became afraid of the size of the sky.

When I think about that moment, my mind goes blank and I can't remember what happened after, nothing until I found myself walking around the judge's garden, holding his hand, not wanting to say painful things that could result in more pain.

At the time my mother lost us, I didn't want to leave her. She made such a scene of grief when our father drove off with us, and she kept crying whenever we met her the odd Saturday, so I felt really sorry for her. At my father's house, I lay under my brother John's bed howling exactly like a wolf from one end of the day to the other until we got sent back. I also spent a lot of time singing "Bohemian Rhapsody" along with the record really loud because Freddie Mercury is singing to his mother.

My father is not a happy person. I can't say I blame him. His voice sounds sad, like an opera singer's, when he sings in the bathroom in the mornings. He gets blue and goes to bed after lunch a lot. I sit next to him at the table and see the sadness come up into his eyes from down inside his belly. He doesn't like me to see it.

He's a bit like someone who has been scalded and is running around looking for cool water to stand under. He can't sit still. He's addicted to working. He gets away with leaving my stepmother to deal with us savages because he's a man. I can't say I blame him for that. I'd try getting away with it too if I were him.

I'm extremely uncomfortable around him. I sit cross-legged on the very edge of my seat and shake my foot really fast without meaning to. I don't really know him and he doesn't really know me. It's not his fault or mine, it's my mother's, because she didn't let him see us for so long. But she didn't tell us she wouldn't let him, so I thought he just didn't come and I was really angry at him inside myself all that time. I get cross if he tells me what to do and I say really nasty stuff like he hasn't any right to act the father now. I'm not a nice person. I'm trouble. I drive him nuts.

Poor guy drops me at school and I just walk out the other gate. I go to the bowling alley and play Pac-Man, waiting for the boys from

Oatlands to come by at lunchtime because I'm in love with B. but he doesn't want a girlfriend, so I'm going out with Jerome Kearns. I don't give a shit about school. What's the point? The most important thing to be doing is getting hugs and Jerome is really nice to me. All we do is talk about Bob Dylan and Pink Floyd and hug. His shoulders are just the right height for my head and he calls me sweet names.

I do turn up for English class when I know we're going to write about Yeats poems. I love Yeats's poems, they're like music but they open up a different sky, the one that's inside me. I'm not scared of that sky because it has boundaries. It feels like the poems have opened all the windows and brought the garden indoors. Now I can see inner scenes, and the outside colors have gone.

There isn't a scary spinning universe outside me; there's a misted olden-days sitting room inside me, with a huge gray marble fireplace. Yeats is out of his mind there, writing "Easter, 1916," about the tragic uprising by Irish Republicans against the British. *Nobody is fucking laughing now* is what I wrote on my test in answer to the question *What was the poet saying?*

Yeats has made me wanna write songs but I ain't ready yet. I haven't fallen in love as many times as him, the silly old bugger. Always asking a woman to marry him and not getting the message when she said no and then asking her daughter, which makes you know why the mother said no so many times. He's a freak. He looks a bit like a walrus. He's quite off-putting. But his poems are paintings. My favorite is "No Second Troy," although I get fed up with people rhyming *desire* with either *fire* or *pyre*. There's got to be some other option.

I've actually been thrown out of, like, three schools in the past nine months. And I still keep getting caught stealing. If a thing ain't nailed down, I'm stealing it. I don't even know why. It's gotten so bad my stepmother called in a social worker, Irene. I hate her. I got caught stealing a pair of gold shoes for my friend to wear to the Pretenders concert. I stole outfits for my friends because I'm the second-fastest sprinter in the class. I just put the clothes on in the shops and run. Irene told my father and my stepmother to send me off to this place I'm now on the way to in my father's car, looking at my own two eyes in the window. Knowing they're the same eyes I'll see all my life.

The place is called An Grianán — "the Sunrise."

THE HOUSE OF THE RISING SUN, PART TWO

WHEN YOU DRIVE in the gates of High Park to An Grianán, there's a massive full-color statue of Jesus in His red and white robes. He has His arms wide open in welcome. I feel sorry for Him — He must be freezing. And I wonder why He always looks like He came from Kerry instead of Bethlehem. Surely His skin and eyes should be browner.

This is a gray place where loads of nuns live. And a lot of old ladies are shuffling around in their slippers with their chins to their chests, but we aren't allowed to talk to them. They live in a different part of the building.

It's a huge building in an L shape. There's a little garden and a big church. I snuck in there once for a funeral to see what a dead nun looked like. The half-moons of her nails were dark purple.

The girls keep saying there's a White Lady ghost in the garden; they say she crosses the little bridge toward the church, but I've never seen her. They also say there's a load of graves covered up with weeds and they're each marked MAGDALEN. But how could so many people in one place have the same name?

I wonder if those old nuns know.

The rule here about music is that you may play two songs on the record player during break time but you have to let the staff know in

53

the morning whether you want to so you can book your slot. That way everyone who wants to gets a turn. The morning I got here, the girls were playing Elkie Brooks's "Don't Cry Out Loud" over and over in the sitting room. It made me crouch down and keen in the corner.

My cubicle has three wooden walls painted pale blue. It has a little dressing table and a chair and a little bed. Across what should be the fourth wall, an orange flowery curtain blows. When I'm in my bed I can see someone's forgotten a tiny blue-and-white Virgin Mary statue; it's stuck into the latticework above the railings.

When I first got here, the girl in the cubicle next to me used to stick her head over the top of the wall that separates us and smile like a nosy fairy above the blue sky. She wanted to know everything about me. Asked me questions like a machine gun's rat-a-tats. Couldn't find things out quick enough. She likes me. She's real ladylike. She's seventeen. She has dainty little hands and she used to be always shaping her nails. Her nails were perfect. She has dark skin and huge brown eyes and her black hair is cut real short. She looks like Audrey Hepburn, only she's brown. She used to pluck her eyebrows all the time and wear a little lip gloss. She used to speak real ladylike too. If you told her she looked beautiful on a particular day, she'd say, "I know!"

I think all the girls are here because their families don't want them. One plays Supertramp's "The Logical Song" over and over. If I were her mother or father, she wouldn't be here or anywhere listening to such a sad song. One has a crooked hip; she needs operations. She's had loads already but she's waiting to grow up some more before she can have the next big one. I don't know why she isn't waiting with her family. She's only twelve and she's a traveler.

Her cousin is here too. She's really pretty. She's a traveler too. She has lovely black hair and dark yellow skin. She's about seventeen, I guess. She is the most beautiful girl God ever made. I love how the two of them talk; their accent is so beautiful and their voices are so deep.

The way they use words is not like regular people. I practice talking like them in my cubicle because I love how they talk so much. When I get it right, it feels the same as singing.

One of the girls is twenty-two. Word is she's been here since she was my age, fourteen. That scares me; I don't want to be here when I'm twenty-two. She doesn't seem completely "present." She has the same look in her eyes and the same way of shuffling about in her slippers as those old ladies.

She slightly talks to herself, like old women do. And licks her lips too much. No one ever comes to visit her. In fact, very rarely does anyone's family come. When someone's parents visit, whichever girl it is goes downstairs to the tiny side sitting room by the front door and there's tea and it's all very polite. Sometimes the parents take the girl out, but they always bring their daughter back. I'm always hoping they won't. I hope they'll run with their child and forget all about this sad place, but they don't.

One skinny girl is really angry, but I like her, although she's extra-scary because she'll tell you to go fuck yourself and look like a wolf when she says it, with fangs and everything. She laughs at me a lot, in a cruel way. I don't like that, but still, there's something about her I admire. I wish I were brave enough to be as rude as her. She says all the bad things she thinks. I burst mine out only when I'm really hurt and lose my temper.

She's getting an office job. They brought us to buy her some office-looking clothes. I felt sad for her when she turned her face away to lean against the door of the old-fashioned Gresham Hotel while we took a break from shopping after I said something that accidentally made her feel something other than fury. It took her ages to make herself look violent again. She isn't violent at all; she's a canary in a tiger suit.

Upstairs they teach us typing in the afternoons but in the mornings, we do math and English and other lessons with John. I really like him. Actually, I have a massive crush on him because he's gentle and I like the sound of his voice. But I still pay no attention unless we're studying poems or short stories. Then I'm pretty sure I can see him secretly thinking, *Hmm, maybe that annoying girl isn't totally pointless after all*. It's like a quick eureka moment for him. Gone as soon as the math book comes out and I prove impossible.

Sometimes people come round on a Friday night to sing with us, trainee priests and such. "Good people" earning brownie points with God by hanging out with the bad kids. I fell in love with one of the trainee priests, another John. (I always fall in love with people called John.) This John is gentle, like teacher John. (As I've said, I always fall in love with gentle people.) This John loves God as much as I do and he likes to talk about nothing but God and songs, so I thought, *He's perfect*, and I asked him to forget about becoming a priest and marry me instead, but he said no.

At this rate I'm never gonna get married. I keep getting turned down.

One night a band called the Fureys played a gig downstairs in our little concert hall. We girls were allowed to attend. They played my favorite song, "Sweet Sixteen," which always makes me think of my first love, B. I had to leave him when I came here, him and all my other friends. But then they did an instrumental piece, played on a sort of high Irish whistle, that they said Finbar Furey, the lead singer, wrote when he was twelve. It was called "The Lonesome Boatman." The most beautiful and haunting melody I've ever heard. Such grief to have come from a child. It was like he knew my own heart. And no one in this place had ever known my heart.

I waited behind when the audience left and the band was packing up. Walked up to Finbar and told him he'd made me want to be a musician.

I'm friends with him now (at fifty-three years of age) and he doesn't remember meeting me. But I will always remember meeting him. And to this day, if I so much as see his name on a dressing-room door, as I sometimes do when we are doing the same festivals, I cry. Just because his music and his songs are so beautiful.

• • •

When you get to nearly eighteen, they start setting you up for a job. They've been teaching us typing so we can get jobs in typing pools or offices. They start letting you out now and then to get you used to the world of work. You do the odd day in the office or typing pool that you're gonna be working in. When the girl in the cubicle next to mine, the one who looks like a dark Audrey Hepburn, started this process, she met a boy from Glenageary, which is where I'm from. She and this boy fell in love and she got pregnant.

She was very happy about it. And really excited and proud. She was, of course, in trouble with the nuns. The baby was a boy, so white his skin was blue, and his hair was black as night. She fussed over him and took care of him and all his little clothes, just as she had formerly fussed over herself. She adored him.

I loved holding him. I loved his little noises. I loved the smell of her on his little head. He looked like baby Moses, all wrapped up in his blue and white blanket, ready to float up the Nile in his reed basket.

I don't know if she knew they weren't going to let her keep him. I don't know if we knew. But I don't think we did. I got such a shock, is why I can't remember, when they took him from her arms and he was gone. Someone told me that in Ireland, you can't keep your baby if you are under eighteen and not married.

Now she's gone too, even though her body is still here.

She doesn't shape her nails. She doesn't do her makeup. She doesn't dress nice anymore. She never smiles or speaks. All she does is cry her poor heart out all day. She says they didn't give him to his father, and she doesn't know who they gave him to. They just took him and he's gone. Poor lonesome little Moses.

THE HOUSE OF THE RISING SUN,
PART THREE

THERE WERE MAYBE four hospital beds against each wall, with curtains drawn around them. Just like a real hospital. Everything was colored buttermilk — the linoleum, the curtains, the walls. The lights were very low and dark yellow and seemed to shine from behind the walls so that they leaked up the back of the cubicles. Since no staffers were present, I stood waiting, expecting someone to come and say where I should sleep. I heard moaning from one of the beds; someone was calling, "Nurse, nurse." After ten minutes no one came so I stole a quick peek into each cubicle. Every bed had in it an ancient lady, sleeping. I'd been in hospitals before and seen some dying people, so I recognized this was a tiny hospice. And I recognized these were some of the old ladies I sometimes saw shuffling about the grounds, the ladies we were never allowed to talk to.

I'd been sent up here to sleep by Sister Margaret as punishment for the most recent of several successful escapes, all of which had resulted in much busking and entering of talent shows at hotels around Dublin, where I would always win the fiver if I sang "Don't Cry for Me Argentina." The final time I ran away I made a big mistake — I brought another girl with me. An older girl. She ended up shagging a guy against the wall of a block of flats, and his friends ran off with all our stuff, so I got scared and went back to Grianán. The girl didn't come back for about two weeks. I never saw my stuff again but luckily I hadn't lost my new guitar because I'd never put it down.

The old ladies don't lift their feet much when they go around the edges of the building, like a row of ducks behind no mother. All seems unnaturally reversed because there is always a nun behind them. The ladies' slippers make a *shh-shh* sound. I get such a strange feeling when I see them, alarmed by the courtyard I can't cross to quiz them. They all hold their chins to their chests and hold their hands clasped across their wombs, and it makes them look as if they've murdered someone and are praying for forgiveness or as if they're a line of slaves in ghostly silent shackles on their way to auction.

I stayed that night in the one bed I found that didn't have anyone in it. All through the night the lady next to me called out in a frightened voice. Other ladies called out sometimes too, but no one came. I rolled, half asleep, half awake, trying to figure out why Sister Margaret had gone to such an extreme; the usual punishment is you are put in Coventry and you have to sleep on your mattress on the floor outside your room and eat on your own. You're not nice again until after all the girls wash their clothes in the laundry before the Wednesday-night meeting.

It's a bit weird in the laundry. For a start, there isn't a washing machine in sight. There are lots of pipes and maybe thirty enormous white sinks and a ton of spiders. It's all made of concrete, and the floor is worn into deep grooves from zillions of footsteps. Looks like the rock at Lourdes, which is worn from a hundred and thirty years' worth of hands that have rubbed it in the hopes of having miracle babies.

At some point I fell asleep and dreamed the old lady in the cubicle next to me was sitting on my bed, lighter of demeanor and seeming years younger, shaping her nails and singing "I Don't Know How to Love Him." And then the walls and curtains of the cubicles vanished and the old ladies' beds became rows of graves marked MAGDALEN.

• • •

I never ran away again after my night in the hospice. In the morning when I woke, I knew what Sister Margaret had been trying to tell me. The worst part was, I knew she wasn't being unkind. She was being a nun I'd never seen before. She deliberately hadn't told me why I was to go to a part of the building I'd never known existed, climb a flight of stairs I would never have been allowed to ascend if I'd asked to, knock on a door I would previously not have been permitted to touch, and enter such a scene with no staff present.

She let me figure it out for myself—if I didn't stop running away, I would someday be one of those old ladies.

Some months after I came to Grianán, I noticed one of the senior girls was allowed to go outside to school because she was doing her leaving-cert. So she was having a life. I managed to talk my father and Sister Margaret into letting me go to the school across the road to do my inter-cert. I wasn't entirely lying when I told them I wanted to write about the poems and the stories, and we never had enough time with John to study them, but my main objective was not to end up a nun or a locked-up old lady or working in a typing pool or having to be a "housewife."

It was partly Sister Margaret's fault I'd kept running away; she shouldn't have bought me that guitar. When she brought me to the shop, I chose an acoustic steel-string so I could be like my big brother, Joe. As she was paying, I browsed the shelves and found a book of Bob Dylan's songs with lyrics and pictures of how to play the chords. I made her throw it in. She said she'd get a teacher to come in if I would like, and one day along came this lovely lady called Jeanette who spoke with a very English accent and was therefore neither square nor boring. She showed me how to figure out from the pictures of the chords what my fingers were supposed to do. The first song I learned to play was "To Ramona."

Ramona, come closer
Shut softly your watery eyes
The pangs of your sadness
Will pass as your senses will rise
The flowers of the city
Though breathlike,
Get deathlike at times
And there's no use in tryin'
T' deal with the dyin'
Though I cannot explain that in lines

I stuck around for only like two or three lessons before I started running away. Being the drama kid, flapping about with sore fingers, making music in parks from pictures in my book. Flying over to see my mother occasionally too. I was "got" once from my mother's. Always had to come back after like twenty-four hours. Nowhere else to go. On the few occasions when I was not brought back, I would tramp back and lie a lot upon return if I hadn't been supposed to see my mother or if I'd stolen stuff while AWOL (which of course I had) or if I needed to protect someone, such as my brother's friend who let me stay the night on his office floor and who would consequently have been slaughtered if anyone found out.

Sister Margaret tried to break the hold my mother had on me. That was the toughest job for her because she couldn't get to me at all. I'd never say a word, just cry totally silent and red-faced, big buckets. After a while she'd come round to my side of the desk and hold me like I was one of her African babies so I could cry into her nice blue nun's blouse and snot upon it, which would make me giggle, and she'd say softly, "Oh, Sinéady."

In the sitting room she'd sing a song from Africa, "Malika." I think she said it meant "angel." She liked singing. She was in Africa when she was a younger nun, for years. But when you're a nun they tell you where to be, and they told her to come back to Ireland. When she talks about it, her eyes go navy with the effort of keeping in her tears. Her face turns to the window as if she's searching for birds. Her job is to mind sad girls and she's a sad girl herself.

I convinced her to buy me a red parka at No Romance, on George's Street; it's a punk-clothes shop. She bought it because I'm leaving. I've done my time, as the song says, I'm getting my life back. Let me rephrase that: I'm getting a life, and she bought me the parka to celebrate. It's so cool. I look like a proper punk girl now. I think she might miss me. She's a bit sniffly.

I don't give a shit about anyone but myself right now, and I'm not sniffly at all. I just want out of here because I want B. to see me in my parka. That's why I wanted it and made Sister Margaret get it. The worst loss was the hope of him when I came here. He has a green parka. It was warm in there with him, only time I ever felt at home apart from Granny's.

I'm allowed to leave because I agreed to go to boarding school. That's the deal. I'm going to my father's house for the summer and then to the boarding school in Waterford. After that I can go to my father's house every second weekend and for the school holidays. My friend says it costs three pounds ten pence for two boiled eggs on the train to Waterford. You could buy a whole flippin' family of chickens for that.

Grianán was full of wild kids. There wasn't one square. I learned a lot about where I was living from them and what everyone thought of us residents. Spent more time in the toilets smoking and chatting with girls equally as punk as me (which wasn't very much at all) than actually in class. Smoking was the only reason to live for those of us who weren't enjoying living, and school was never in our lives a place of education. It was a place of refuge. I got a C in art, a D in some other stuff, and the usual Es, Fs, and NGs in everything else. NG is "no grade." I don't even care.

There ultimately were a few good things about my time at Grianán.

A sweet boy, David, and me fell in love. He was a proper punk. He had the hair and the safety pins and everything. My father said he's not allowed to sit on our furniture. I went to this boy's house a lot. His mother was really kind to me, such a gentle woman. Him too. A lamb. He was really upset about something and nobody could figure out what it was. His mother told me she was worried about him. But me and him had a silly time together; he never seemed upset. He was really happy and his eyes all shone like he was a spaceman and he kissed me awful soft, and his parents in the kitchen next to the sitting room, and me and David played side 1 of *Let's Dance* and made love.

I already know singing is a thing that will take me away from people.

Before I left Grianán, I sang at my guitar teacher Jeanette's wedding. "Evergreen." My knees shook. Jeanette's brother, Paul Byrne, is the drummer in a band called In Tua Nua. Him and the guitar player, Ivan O'Shea, gave me a tape with some music on it. Asked would I write some words for it because they were looking for a singer. Sister Margaret let me come out a few Sundays and they brought me to Eamonn Andrews's studios and I sang with reverb and headphones for the first time. I love reverb so much—it sounds like church. Sister Margaret was pretty cool to have let me do it. I think it's because they said they'd pay me. Not that she wanted the money; she was just glad I could do something other than steal to earn my keep. They kept the song, which was called "Take My Hand," but said I was too young to be their singer. I was so jealous of the girl who got the job that at first I wanted to cry when I heard her sing my words. And she was so gorgeous and beautiful, and, to be fair, she did sing it better. I sounded like a child. She sounded like a woman. A child can't be singing a song whose narrator is Death.

I don't know where it came from.

SONG TO THE SIREN

I LOVE MY STEPMOTHER. She's the sweetest lady on earth. So when I say this, I mean it with kindness: the woman will never give you a lift anywhere. Secretly, I think she's wise. If she starts with one of us, seven more will expect the same. She's Protestant. They're way more practical. They don't have the guilt. She genuinely doesn't care. No amount of big-eyeing or eyelash-batting or crying or foot-stomping or whining will result in you getting dropped off or picked up. Ever. You can sink or sodding swim. So when I saw her car coming toward me down Beechwood Avenue with my stepsister crying in the passenger seat, I knew my mother was dead.

I'd just left my bedsit to walk up the road to my father's house, as was usual on a Sunday. I now share the bedsit with C., my friend who won the Halloween fancy dress last year although she hadn't dressed up. She's having an affair with the singer from the Fine Young Cannibals. Apparently he is fine and young and having her for breakfast, dinner, and tea.

She'd gone to sleep the night before while me and Kevin stayed awake talking. Kevin was my boyfriend, but we're kind of back to being just best friends now. He plays congas. He's lovely and kind to me. He's so good to me, in fact, there aren't words. Doesn't matter if we're going out with each other or not. We just are best friends anyway. So we sit around of a Saturday night, chewing the cud, talking shite.

We wandered into discussing how either of us might react if one or both of our parents died. That's the other reason I knew when I saw my stepmother's car. Blew my mind that something had told us the night before and I was only finding out now.

My younger brother John had been in the car. In my mother's car, not my stepmother's. Luckily he was not physically injured and was released from hospital into the care of my father. He's sixteen.

He'd been in the back seat; there was another man in the passenger seat. He thankfully was not physically injured either. My brother had gone unconscious and woken in hospital to be told his mother was dead. By the time I got to my father's house, he was there, lying in a bed. Or on a sofa—I don't remember exactly. None of us had seen him for ages. He never left my mother. The rest of us did.

To my mother, any of us four entering the house of my stepmother was the ultimate betrayal. My mother never considered that betraying my brother mattered a shred. But the idea of betraying her was a crucifixion to him because he needed her love so much, and he was intensely upset about being where he was now.

Unfortunately my father and my younger brother have a horrible relationship. This is my mother's and my father's fault in equal measure. They used my brother badly. It led to a terrible series of events for which my brother got the blame and in which my father played the victim.

There had been a war between my parents over certain material objects, all of which were sought by my father very aggressively from the time my parents' marriage officially ended, ten years ago. Jewelry in particular. Capodimonte figurines. Portraits. Various other items. My mother hid some of the goods in the attic, others in the bank. Numerous attempts had been made to remove the goods from my mother's possession, none successful.

On the mantelpiece was their wedding photo. My father had torn it down the middle and put it back together in the frame like a jigsaw puzzle.

Everything she'd had on this earth was left to my brothers, so my father had no say in matters concerning her possessions. She's dead, but the war goes on. Clever bitch. She hadn't left my brothers her things because she cared about them; she'd done it to win the war. We were all only collateral to her. That's all we'd ever been. At least, that's how it feels to me.

You wonder how on earth these people ever had sex enough to create four children when they truly hated each other so much.

It was black ice. On the new road they're building in Shankill, by the church. She was driving to Mass. A bus skidded, or she skidded. I don't know. I'm not gonna press my brother on the details. She's dead. And we four were delivered instructions from the funeral home — via my father, via my stepmother — along with fifty pounds to go to Dunnes and buy a dress "which buttons at the neck" to bury her in.

We four kids went to her house. In shock. We rifled through everything in it like crows. In the front garden we set fire to a biscuit tin that we'd loaded up with a literal mountain of Valium from all the bottles we found. She's been eating and drinking it, as they say, for years. She didn't even need a prescription anymore. The chemist just gave it to her.

I haven't got used to putting her in the past tense yet.

In the Dunnes dress shop we laughed hysterically. Crying-laughing. Found it stupidly funny that the sweet girl helping us didn't know we were buying a dress our mother was gonna wear for eternity. The more helpful questions she asked, the more we had to hold ourselves not to pee. Poor girl must have thought we'd been released from the zoo.

I guess we had.

In the church I felt really angry when all the people came to shake our hands. This was the morning before the day of the funeral. We were sitting in the front row. We'd never seen these people when she was alive. I was angry they hadn't helped us. Or her. I didn't know who half of them were. And the ones I knew made me feel angrier. They'd known. Not the details. But they'd known. And they hadn't done a thing but came now to shake our hands and tell us how sorry they were for our loss. I was tempted to ask, *Which loss in particular?* But I didn't want to upset my big brother, Joe, any more than he was already. We've more chance of actually raising our mother from the dead some Easter Sunday than ever getting back what we really lost. Which is ourselves, years before now.

I screamed at God in the sky last night. Called Him all the cruel bastards under the sun until I puked. It hurt real bad, to say hateful things to Him. It's not the first time I've done it.

His answers are always silent. It took me a while to come to grips with that. I got annoyed in the early days. I thought the silence meant He didn't care. So I'd scream more until I was all screamed out and could only be silent myself. I thought you were supposed to hear His voice like in all the stories. I found out the fact is that He can't speak because He's crying so much Himself. Who can speak when they're weeping?

In the funeral home, my father cried over my mother's body. Said, "I'm sorry, Marie," over and over. That made me angry too. Why sorry now and not before? Why no "I'm sorry" from either of them to the four of us? Why conduct a war and then say "Sorry" when someone is dead? I ran away, out of the funeral home. Down the road through Glasthule and into Dun Laoghaire. I don't think I'll ever stop running. I don't know how I'll ever not be angry. Nothing is ever gonna be fixed now.

The next day as we were waiting in my father's sitting room for the funeral cars, I decided to smoke myself to death. Decided that I would smoke and smoke all my life, as many cigarettes as it took to send me to my mother. I can't remember anything from the funeral but feet around the grave. I looked down. We all did. Crying.

Sinéad with her sister, Éimear

SISTERS

MY SISTER, ÉIMEAR (pronounced "Eeemer"), is barely fourteen months older than me. But she has always been a mother as well as a sister to me.

We shared the same bed growing up. We had an imaginary line down the middle. And God help whichever one of us crossed the line accidentally or on purpose. We'd be kicking the crap out of each other. We did a lot of that, like a pair of boys.

But if the shit hit the fan, Éimear would instantly switch into mother mode. For example, one Christmas morning at my father's house, where we shared a room with two single beds in it, she and I had a fight and she stomped on my chocolate Santa, so I quite rightly gave her an unmerciful kick in the butt and ran for the door, her chasing after me. Only I twisted my ankle before I escaped and fell screaming in pain. In a millisecond, Éimear was all like "Oh my God, are you okay?" and down on the floor beside me, argument forgotten. She loves me. I don't know why. But she does.

For one reason and one reason alone, it was hell sharing that bedroom in my father's house with her: she was in love with Barry Manilow. So her side of the room was papered with massive posters of him while mine was all Siouxsie and the Banshees. Each of us woke in hell, I would imagine, if my posters scared her in the night as much as her talking about Manilow in romantic terms scared me.

Previously, she'd been in love with Daniel Boone. Now that, I could understand. But not Manilow. But then, she and I, thank God, have never liked the same kind of men. I like punks and bad boys. She likes boring good boys.

She never got in trouble with our father. Which really pissed me off. I was always in trouble. Sometimes I called my father pretending to be Éimear because he couldn't tell the difference between our voices and I'd get to find out what consequences were in store for Sinéad when she got home.

We still love smashing chocolate because of the Santa episode, so every year at Christmas we stomp on a couple of chocolate Santas, and at Easter we smash up beautiful chocolate chickens with a hammer. We started that tradition when she was going through a breakup. She was crying in my kitchen and it was Easter and, well, someone had given someone a chocolate chicken in a basket, so I just handed her a hammer. She laughed through her tears while beating the thing to smithereens.

Though Éimear never got in trouble, it's not that she wasn't up to mischief. It's just she never got caught like me. At school she was a prefect. Made life hell for me and my little gang, who were all the "bad" girls. She'd be chasing us and I would stop and make a square shape with my hand, calling her a square. Used to drive her crazy. But she is square compared to me. And I'm jealous. I secretly long to be square. It ain't comfy being squ-oval.

Today she is a doctor of art history. Very smart. And she doesn't suffer fools for one minute. She had a store years ago in which she sold her own paintings, which were gorgeous. She put the door on the store by herself. Huge door, and she managed to screw in all the hinges. And she's half the weight of myself. She always thinks she's fat. But she ain't at all.

How she is different from me is that she has red hair and self-esteem. I don't have either. She makes me say affirmations—"I am loving. I am lovable. I love and accept myself" et cetera—in the mirror. It doesn't work, but being around her makes me like myself better. Because she likes me, and she doesn't like anyone who doesn't like me. She has no mental illness. She's never been a pain in the arse. She isn't difficult or too emotional like I am. She isn't vengeful like me. She has no mean streak. She can walk away from abuse without becoming abusive. I wish I were like her in those ways. Lord knows I'm working on it.

Not long ago, she came to visit me in the hospital. She held my hand and walked me through the garden of the hospital saying, "I love you." Suddenly it felt like we were little kids again. We had tramped the streets of Dublin together as children—Moore Street, Parnell Street. We'd go to the Kingfisher chip shop with money we'd begged from strangers by telling them we needed to buy a bus ticket home. Fact is, we were doing everything we could to *avoid* home. (This is when we lived with our mother.) We did anything to stay out because only battering would happen at home. Some nights we just rode the bus from the first stop to the last and back in the hope that Mother would be asleep when we got home. We were a strange mixture: middle-class kids with filthy clothes that had not been washed for years, begging. We were good at begging; we had to be or we would have starved. In summer, when all the kids were happy going home, we hid our field hockey sticks at school and cried. We knew we were in for weeks of violence. The other kids expected weeks of joy, their mothers smiling. Ours was frothing at the mouth. No rescuer in sight. No respite. Only the certainty of doom.

ANY DREAM WILL DO

MY BROTHER JOSEPH and I have a similar relationship as my father and I do in that we get along only when discussing music. Rest of the time, my brother doesn't like me. Because I'm a pain in the ass and too emotional. But when we were growing up, he was my hero. I used to walk around carrying his empty guitar case so I'd look cool like him. Though he went through a phase of wanting to be a priest, he wisely became a writer instead. And wrote, in fact, one of my two favorite novels of all time, *Redemption Falls* (my second favorite is *Mistaken*, by Neil Jordan).

I've probably spent a total of an hour with him since I was eighteen and our mother died. It is hard for children of abuse to be around each other. Triggers and reminders. Plus I lost my shit with him maybe once too often. Plus he lost his shit with me once too often. We are bad-tempered, the O'Connors. It's sad, really. We didn't get set an example of blood being thicker than water. I'm sure in our veins there's not blood, but water.

Joe plays guitar. He says he doesn't play well, but he does. My sister plays harp and my younger brother plays drums. I always thought it would be brilliant to make one album together and call it *Fuck the*

Corrs. But the fights would have made Liam and Noel Gallagher seem like pussycats.

He's funny, my brother Joe. Pants-pissingly funny. I miss him very much. And I feel shit about myself because we are so distant. But he is still my hero. And I love him to my soul.

JOHN, I LOVE YOU

MY LITTLE BROTHER, John, is two years younger than me. My mother gave him a very hard time. The nights I heard him scream for mercy (at her command) and couldn't rescue him have vastly contributed to my activism and my anger-management problem. I couldn't save him. I couldn't protect him. I couldn't even move a muscle to get myself from my room to his. I have been angry at my mother all my life. But I displaced it. I couldn't admit it was her I was angry at, so I took it out on the world. And burned nearly every bridge I ever crossed.

If I could go back in time and flatten my mother or have her arrested, I would. But I can't. Neither myself nor John came out of what happened to us quite as well adjusted as my older siblings. We didn't get the same self-esteem lessons Joe and Éimear had. All we got were the lessons from our mother about what a ruination of her life we were. She humiliated John in front of us and humiliated us in front of him. Many's the time I confessed to doing something I hadn't done so that she wouldn't beat John for it. I'd take the beating instead.

I know Éimear feels the same way about me. Not being able to rescue me hurt her. Just as not being able to rescue John hurt me.

Once when we were teenagers, John and I went to the cinema to see the horror movie *Halloween*. The murderer was wearing a white hockey goaltender mask. Afterward, John chased me all the way up O'Connell

77

Street with his white motorbike helmet on backward. How he didn't bash into anything I'll never know. He scared the bejaysus out of me.

Once I bit his nose during a pretend fight. The clever fucker snotted into my mouth.

We really are a very messed-up family. We don't even suit that word, *family*. It should be a comforting word. But it's not. It's a painful, stabbing word. Cuts the heart into pieces. And all the more because it's too late to go back and do anything differently.

ABOUT MY DAD

I TRIED TO SCORE some hash when I was about fifteen but it never turned up. Largely because the dude I gave the fiver to died. And no, it wasn't my father who killed him.

The dude was an associate of my stepsister, and my father knew he was up to no good. Dude was lurking on the path outside my father's front garden one night, peering over the hedge, waiting for my stepsister to come out. My father spied him and lured him into the garden with talk of "She'll be out in a minute, come on in," then knocked him flat out on the grass with one punch to the side of his head. He was tall and lanky. My father is five foot four, like me.

Dude had the utter gormlessness (this is an Anglo-Irish word for stupidity of the sort that would have Bill Clinton in the Oval Office with a cigar and Monica Lewinsky) to come back another night, believing my father to be out. At the time, my little brother was young enough to have a tricycle. It was sitting in the tiny red-tiled porch outside the front door. Soon as my father spotted the dude, he grabbed the tricycle, ran with it to the gate, hopped onto it, and chased the guy down the road, his knees nearly hitting his face with each push of the pedals. Poor dude ran for dear life for miles, looking over his shoulder every few seconds with such an expression of sheer horror, you'd think Freddy Krueger was after him.

When my big brother was little, a dog was bothering him at school every morning. After a few weeks of no change in the situation, my father went in with my brother to locate the dog. Dog starts snarling at Joe. My father gives it one Francis Street kick. Dog never went near Joe again. You do *not* wanna mess with my father. I'm like him, I guess.

At school once, when me and my sister were about five and six, respectively, we cornered a poor girl who had dared to state that her father was better-looking than ours. Since our father was the handsomest man on earth, we weren't having her nonsense, so we made her take it back. Not that we were gonna hurt her, and we didn't make any specific threat or anything; we just declared our absolute rejection of her assessment of the situation and then towered over her silently until she recanted. We proudly informed our father later that his honor and reputation had been defended.

I ought to mention, if I have not already, my father's impressive and inspiring humility. Of which I hope to have at least one drop.

At eighty-two, he's retired, of course, from his occupation as a construction engineer. But he still lifts me up when I am down. He makes me feel tall again when I feel small. I love him very much and I regret all the years I didn't speak with him because I was young and stupid. I would advise any young person not to do what I did. Time passes quickly and you can't get it back.

But we are with each other now and that is the greater blessing of both our lives.

POEM FROM MY YOUTH

The child who has been speaking isn't speaking now
If you dance with me I let you fall asleep
Further when you sleep with me you don't need dreams
If you don't know who to be, you can be me

I am the one whose hand she took but I don't like labels.
Some call me music, some the great absolver
I sat with her when she thought I was a cloudy spirit
I took her for myself because I love her

Why? A sensitive girl, we don't want to lose her.
Rarely has somebody got faith like her.
She asked for help and I did overhear
her say, "I only want to disappear"

I put my hands about her little waist
Dark blue and green and red sparkles my face
I flung her and I spun her round the place
I shone upon her and she vanished into space

PART TWO

Teenage entrepreneur
COURTESY OF THE AUTHOR

WHO ARE YOU?

BEST DAY OF MY LIFE was the day I first left Ireland, and any other day I left Ireland was the next best.

Happened to be someone up there likes me, so in 1985, a fortnight or so after we buried my mother (don't worry, we made sure she was dead first), Ensign Records got in touch with me via a guy named Ciaran Owens whom I had met while singing with Ton Ton Macoute, a band I'd joined the previous summer. It was named after the Haitian secret police, a terrible name chosen by the bandleader and bass player, Colm Farrelly, who fancied himself something of a witch.

I'd put an advert in *Hot Press*, Ireland's only music magazine, saying I was a singer looking for a band. I'd tramped about the suburbs of Dublin auditioning in people's garages and sitting rooms, settling finally on Ton Ton because it didn't seem likely to be a square situation, musically speaking, whereas the others had—Colm's utter madness being the deciding factor.

He'd also agreed we could do some of my songs, while the other bands had not. The other bands would have had me singing "Summertime" for the rest of my life and I'd rather have poked my own eyes out.

Ton Ton lasted about a year. The big-shot record executive Nigel Grainge and Chris Hill of Ensign were inclined to scout Ireland for acts because they'd had the Boomtown Rats and Thin Lizzy. Ciaran Owens was one of their go-to guys for advice on what was hot or not round town. He had taken them to a gig of ours six months previously.

Now they'd tracked me down through Ciaran and called me. Said they wanted me to come to London to make some demos with Karl Wallinger from the Waterboys and asked how soon could I do so. They said they didn't want the band, just me, which suited me fine because we'd some weeks previously discovered that Colm had been squirreling away any money we earned for himself and so the band had broken up.

I jumped on a plane within forty-eight hours of Ensign calling me with the help of a hundred quid kindly offered to me by the lovely boss of the restaurant where I was working, the Bad Ass Café in Dublin, where myself and all the other waitresses wore white T-shirts that said NICE PIZZA ASS. (I kid you not, I actually didn't realize what it meant until I was about twenty-eight.)

I demoed four songs with Karl, three of which eventually made it onto my first album, *The Lion and the Cobra*. The first was a song called "Drink Before the War," which I'd written the previous year about my constipated headmaster who hated me making music and campaigned for my father not to let me take my guitar with me back to boarding school, despite the fact that all I could do was make music. I used to smoke right outside his gate to try to get expelled as a protest against his protest against my music-making. It never worked. One morning he bawled me out in front of the whole assembly at school. He was an unmerciful snob. "If you're going to make music," he whined down his pompous nose, "you're going to spend the rest of your life going in the back door." Pronouncing the last two words as if their literal meaning was "dog shit." He didn't know going in the back door was the whole point. To him, fun was public enemy number one.

There was a reason he was so angry: One of my teachers, a glorious black-bearded music-loving man by the name of Joe Falvey, had a friend who had a recording studio in Cork, which was quite a drive from Waterford, where our school was. Me and my friend Jeremy had been busking with our guitars around Waterford and earned ourselves quite the reputation, so several times, Mr. Falvey drove us to Cork, where we recorded all night and then sneaked back to school. And we'd all got caught.

Me and Jeremy had been busking on the weekends and after school too. There was even a pub where we'd started doing gigs. So we weren't at all concentrating on our studies. We couldn't have given a toss. Neither could Mr. Falvey. But the headmaster wasn't having it. We were bringing the school into rock 'n' roll disrepute.

One Friday morning after a few weeks of failing to get expelled, I woke and realized the first class of that day was double home economics. I didn't want to be a housewife. I didn't like what I'd seen of it. I hated cooking. And besides, I wanted to sleep with more than one man.

I asked my friend Hugh to help me get the train back to Dublin that morning. I can't remember if he drove or how we got to the station, but he helped me get my stuff together and put me on the train.

I went to Colm's house. He was older than the rest of us in Ton Ton Macoute, but he lived with his old mother. I stayed with him a few nights and got some money from him to rent a room at a place in Dublin called Dolphin's Barn.

I didn't contact my father for about a week. When I did, he took it well. He realized I had my mind made up. And I'd gotten a job as well as joined a band. He was clever; he gave me two hundred pounds a month, which was exactly enough to pay my rent and no more, so I couldn't sit on my ass and not work if I wanted to eat or pay my bills. Not that I would have anyway. But it was really clever.

There was a bricklayer, a huge guy, living in the room above me. I had to borrow twenty quid from him once. When I was late paying him back, he broke into my room while I was out and stole all my stuff. Including a flute my friend Barbara had given me. I moved.

All the band did was rehearse all day, every day, apart from work hours, and all night too, at the few pub gigs or talent contests we'd do. We had a space up top of an old building on Crown Alley, and the place I worked was on the same street. All the pizza I could eat. And all the chefs I could seduce. Then all the singing I could do.

I also got a job as a kissogram girl. Twenty-five quid was what some idiot would pay me to turn up in a French maid outfit, say a stupid poem in a dreadful French accent, and place a pair of French frilly knickers on some poor dude's head. It being Ireland, of course there was no actual kissing, despite the job title.

I got paid six pounds out of the twenty-five. My friend Barbara (who gave me the flute that was later stolen) was married to Steve Wickham, a violin player with both In Tua Nua and the Waterboys. She asked me one day if she too could be a kissogram girl because she was a bit bored. She was an American from Atlanta, so she was braver than me, and she was gorgeous and outgoing and blond. The dude who ran the company, which was called Hot Lips, took full advantage and had her wear a bikini with balloons that the guys could bite tied around the bra and knickers.

I was slightly envious. But then I would get to wear my favorite outfit, which was "the Naughty Nun," a full habit from head to toe at the front, nothing at the back from the waist down, and fishnet stockings and stilettos.

It felt so wrong but it felt so right.

I was the worst kissogram girl who ever lived, I reckon. I was very shy. And the poems, composed by the dude who ran the company, were embarrassingly bad. I'd shake reading them and run as soon as they were uttered.

The dude who ran the company also did gorillagrams and Tarzans for the ladies. He lived in what seemed to be a former boys' home run by priests. The house was now inhabited by one elderly priest and several young men. There was a large statue of a pale blue and white Virgin Mary in the glass archway above the front door. The guy had a red car with a giant pair of red lips on top. We went driving around Deansgrange Cemetery in it once, looking for my mother's grave, may the Lord have mercy on us, he in his gorilla suit, me in my French maid's outfit, giggling like idiots.

• • •

Next song I demoed for Ensign that made it onto my first album was "Just Like U Said It Would B," which Steve Wickham played on. That was about a lesson I'd been having from a certain minister on the art and outcomes of praying Psalm 91, which is where my album's title is taken from.

Next, there was "Never Get Old," another song I had written at school, about a very quiet boy all the girls were secretly in love with. He had a hawk. He took me out to the fields once and showed me. He let me wear his leather glove and feed the bird bits of raw meat. He was a very gentle-hearted boy.

On the basis of the demos, I was offered a record deal, which I signed on August 5, 1985. The lawyer Ensign had sent me to begged me to let him find me a better deal. But I wasn't taking any risks. I was happy enough. I just wanted to get out of Ireland and be financially independent as quickly as possible, and I wasn't hanging around waiting for another opportunity. I signed for seven points, which means you get paid 7 percent of what your records sell and you pay for pretty much everything to do with recording and promoting and touring out of that 7 percent.

The lawyer's duty was to read me each clause of the contract to make sure I understood it. But I was eighteen, and when you're eighteen, contracts are so boring. Just before my eyes finally glazed over, he had, in all seriousness, talked me through a clause that stated that if and/or when records could be released on the moon, the terms of my contract would apply on the moon. He'd asked if I understood this and I'd drifted off.

There was nothing in my head after that besides a vision of the poor American flag flying in lonesome black and white on the moon. I was thinking it would much rather come home and live on Earth in color, eating burgers and hot dogs, than have records sent up to make its loneliness worse because no one would be there to dry its tears when it heard This Mortal Coil's cover of "Song to the Siren."

The day I'd left Ireland for good, a few weeks previous to signing the contract, Pete Townshend was on my plane. In those days the Aer Lingus planes had pairs of seats facing each other, like trains do. He was sitting opposite me. Either the Who had played in Ireland or there had been some massive gig he'd been attending. I had made my mind up before boarding the flight that I wouldn't even look behind me out the window when we took off. I took Townshend's presence as a sign I had chosen the right path and focused on his face as we slipped toward heaven. I hated Dublin. Everything reminded me of my mother. The shops were full of hats she would have loved but I could never now give her.

At Heathrow there were always two Special Branch men in suits at the end of the gangway when you got off the plane from Ireland, one on the left, one on the right, standing behind black podiums just as you entered baggage reclaim. They stopped only men, specifically men with scruffy-looking beards and long hair. This is because there was a time in the early 1980s that the Northern Ireland hunger strikers were hairy and so was everyone in the IRA. The other side didn't have beards at all, and they didn't have much hair because they were always shouting. They'd all been killing each other up there since as far back as I could remember. It was horrible on the news, fire and blood, and kids and old people screaming in the streets. And shit all over the prison walls and hollow-eyed skinny men whose coffins were so light, they could have been carried by one small child. And gunmen at funerals and men torn from cars there and killed. Through it all, Margaret Thatcher's hair was always perfectly set.

I'd made one or two visits to London in the month or so before I finally left Ireland, between which a savvy Irish music accountant tracked me down by phone at my Dublin bedsit to offer his services. I'd never heard of him or even of such a thing as an accountant. "Oh," he says, "you'll need someone to manage your money for you and I also have the perfect manager for you. Fachtna Ó Ceallaigh, who used to manage the Boomtown Rats."

I'd actually met Fachtna five years previously, when I was thirteen. It was in the foyer of Dublin's Four Courts one afternoon during the time the Rats were being prevented from performing live in Dublin. On the same day as a hearing in a case between my parents, there also happened to be a hearing in the case of the Rats.

My brother Joseph became starstruck on seeing Fachtna walking through the hall to go out the front doors for a smoke, and he jumped up to ask for an autograph. Beaming, he then walked Fachtna over to me and said simply, "This is my little sister." I remember our handshake as if it happened only half an hour ago.

I had two meetings with the accountant before I finally left Ireland, during both of which he drove me insane by repeatedly insisting we "should run all this" (the details of my record and publishing contracts) by my father before I signed. Despite this, I liked the accountant enormously; I found myself having to inform him over and over, each time in a slightly louder voice, that I was eighteen, thank you very much, and no longer my father's concern, and the fact of my being female didn't mean I hadn't understood the contracts when my lawyer sat down and explained them to me. He mistook my indignation for concern that my father should not have to worry about me. In reality, my granny had impressed upon me several times that a woman must never reveal her cash stash to any male relative.

Next time I shook Fachtna Ó Ceallaigh's hand, I was settling myself into a wobbly chair opposite him at a café in Marylebone High Street in London. As he cut around his egg yolks with the point of his knife, I reminded him we had met once before, but of course he didn't remember.

When I got back to Dublin he sent me a card with a note, in lovely Irish-looking writing, saying he was happy to have met me. He was sure I would do well in music and he wanted me to know I should always be myself no matter what the business of music might wish me to be. It hadn't crossed my mind to be anything else, but it later did help having a grown-up who would stand up for one's right, for example, not to have one's eyebrows plucked for a photo session. Or one's right to keep one's top on when a certain European gentleman was the photographer. (This after one had been foolish enough to fall into the trap of removing one's top in the first place because said photographer had phrased it like a challenge. "Do you *mind* taking your top off?" he'd said to an Irishwoman. I'd felt I had to do it to say, *Eff you for even asking.*)

I stayed at my aunt Martha's house in South London for my first few months in London and got to know my two male cousins. One was girl-dressing but straight with long dyed-red hair, the coolest guy on earth. The other had short curly blond hair and was the other coolest guy on earth. They took me clubbing and to shop on the King's Road for a peach Lycra dress. We watched Live Aid in their mother's garden. We went to Clacton-on-Sea to an all-night Doctor and the Medics concert and I fell asleep with my head way too close to a massive speaker. My girl-dressing cousin took me to Kensington Market and there I beheld a smorgasbord of size 12 patent-leather stilettos for men. England was officially the greatest country on earth.

I also found my first teacher of a spiritual nature.

From the time I turned eighteen, if I was sitting with people I had met only once or twice, I would see in my mind the insides of their houses. I'd see the carpets, the walls, the paintings on the walls, the tiny trinkets on bedside cabinets, the colors of the pots and pans, the stash of private letters, everything. It was as if I were floating about in their rooms.

I felt driven to ask whomever I was with if what I was seeing was accurate, and it always was. I described Ensign Records' previous office when I first met Chris Hill and Nigel Grainge, even though I'd never set foot in it. I didn't think much of seeing things; I just took it for granted. But people would look at me as if they felt I should have something important to tell them, and I didn't, and I got fed up disappointing them. I really wanted to get to the bottom of why it was happening so I could stop it.

My aunt Martha and her sisters shared an interest in psychic studies. I told her about what was happening and she introduced me to a friend of hers, a forty-seven-year-old minister of Greenwich Baptist Church who was also a medium and who trained people in the practice of mediumship. I told him I wanted to learn how to shut down the part of me that was drifting inside people without their permission.

The thing was, it was happening because they weren't inside themselves.

The first step in my training was to say Psalm 91 out loud every day.

Whoever dwells in the shelter of the Most High
will rest in the shadow of the Almighty.
I will say of the Lord, "He is my refuge and my fortress,
my God, in whom I trust."
Surely He will save you
from the fowler's snare
and from the deadly pestilence.
He will cover you with His feathers,
and under His wings you will find refuge;
His faithfulness will be your shield and rampart.
You will not fear the terror of night,
nor the arrow that flies by day,
nor the pestilence that stalks in the darkness,
nor the plague that destroys at midday.
A thousand may fall at your side,
ten thousand at your right hand,
but it will not come near you.
You will only observe with your eyes
and see the punishment of the wicked.
If you say, "The Lord is my refuge,"
and you make the Most High your dwelling,
no harm will overtake you,
no disaster will come near your tent.
For He will command His angels concerning you
to guard you in all your ways;
they will lift you up in their hands,
so that you will not strike your foot against a stone.
You will tread on the lion and the cobra;
you will trample the great lion and the serpent.

"Because he loves Me," says the Lord, "I will rescue him;
I will protect him, for he acknowledges My name.
He will call on Me, and I will answer him;
I will be with him in trouble,
I will deliver him and honor him.
With long life I will satisfy him
and show him My salvation."

While sitting in my room one night I saw a person reflected in the glass cabinet wearing a black hood that was hemmed with two gold bands. Then the lights started flashing on and off and I ran out of there, petrified. The minister said I should have stayed because I was getting a message. I said no, I'd rather not have messages from anyone in a hood.

Once I'd made the final move to London and left my aunt's house, the minister declared his undying love; we had somewhat of an affair. This didn't go down well with my aunt when she figured it out, not only because the minister was married but because I think she liked him too. She was livid. She's never gotten over it, actually. Years later, when I went to a family get-together with one of my sons' dads, she glared at me across the dance floor and kept silently mouthing, *I'll have him, I'll have him*, pointing at him and then at her chest.

The minister had convinced me (since I was young and an idiot) that his wife didn't understand him. I was his true love and all that stuff. After a while I realized I was being duped for the *shtup*. Sitting by myself until our once-weekly hour-long visit, not going out with anyone else, I was like Whitney bloomin' Houston, saving all my love, like a total moron. Soon *I* stopped under-flippin'-standing him too.

The minister arrived one night at the flat I'd rented in Lewisham after leaving my aunt's house. He had a messed-up vacuum cleaner his wife didn't want anymore. He thought I might like it as a present. He'd had the nerve to tell her he knew someone who might want it.

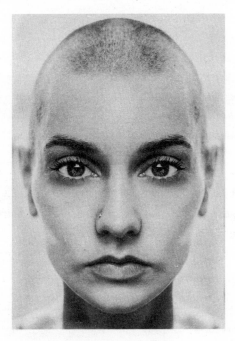

Awaiting her first album's release . . .
KATE GARNER

I considered dropping it on his head from my sixth-floor balcony as I watched him walking to his car.

I got myself a little yellow Fiat Bambino. You could drive in England then with only a provisional license. I'd never had one lesson in my life. I got in the car really late at night and had a crash. Called the minister and said, "I'm hurt, I've crashed my car, will you come get me?" He said no, he wouldn't, because he didn't want anyone to see him with me. I never contacted him again.

I was actually badly hurt. Twisted my pelvis. Got slammed into at full speed by a car on the driver's side. Still have to get straightened out now and then. Right side doesn't move like it should. Walk funny. Walk like Charlie Chaplin. Didn't walk like that before.

95

Nigel Grainge, record company guru
ANDY PARADISE/THE INDEPENDENT/SHUTTERSTOCK

SETTLING IN

THERE ARE ABOUT eight million people in the whole of London. That's twice the entire population of Ireland. I'm finding that a little frightening for the same reason infinity is frightening. It's just too big. The Thames is a hundred times the width of the Liffey.

There are always the lights of planes in the sky. Planes from all over the world always on the way in. Planes only fly past Ireland on their way to somewhere else. Unless they're Irish planes carrying Irish people into and out of the country for amounts of money that increase toward Christmas, the very time anyone who's had the intelligence to leave needs to come back for fear of being a bad son or daughter.

I hate Christmas. I feel pain in my soul like someone drove a tree through my chest.

Apart from my cousins and my aunt, the only people I know in London are Chris and Nigel, from Ensign, and Fachtna, my manager.

I spend a good bit of time at Chris's house. He's really kind and nice to me. He looks after me a lot. I suspect he's slightly in love with me, but he has a wonderful wife he would never disrespect.

Nigel gave me two tapes of Van Morrison songs. I never heard him before. He sounds like one of those Tibetan monks, the kind who use their voices for healing. I get hoovered up by him into some university beyond the veil. It isn't about his words; it's what he does with the sounds of them. He's taken me to where I'm supposed to study. I see beautiful stone buildings, golden-buttressed.

My flat has one sitting room at the front of the building, looking out onto Hither Green Lane. A small bedroom next to it and a small kitchen. It's above an Indian grocery shop. The people down there are nice to me; I was friends with their skinny son who was about my age and into music. We didn't fancy each other or anything, it was just a friendship. We'd just sit and shoot the breeze. I had a record player and he didn't. He could smoke a cigarette away from the wrath of his parents.

He was a very sensitive lad. At some point his father decided he needed toughening up and forced him to join the paratroopers. Poor thing ran up my stairs in a panic with terror in his eyes saying, "What am I gonna do?" There was nothing either of us could do. His father had sprung it on him, and he was to leave the very next day.

About two weeks later I heard my bell ringing in the night. I went to see who was there and it was him! He'd run away. I was filled with pride at his bravery. His face was a picture of shock. Not only from what he'd endured over the fortnight—being screamed at, push-ups, all the usual stuff you see on telly—but from the fact he was defying his father.

He was afraid to go home, so he stayed with me and slept on my sofa for about a week, during which I would go downstairs every day and buy the food we were gonna eat, chatting away with his parents, careful not to mention their son (and they never mentioned him), then back up I'd go. Once he left and went "on the run," I never heard from him again. I didn't live in Hither Green Lane for long after that.

I'm lonely but I'm writing songs for my first album, and songs are a lonely person's occupation; songs are ghosts. When my album comes out I'll become a traveling "ghost delivery woman." There'll be a lifetime of goodbyes. I can't have a problem with that.

I wrote a song called "Troy," about my mother and about the minister. I did the demo vocal in Chris's house. I made him stand outside the door. When I let him back in, he was really shaken. He said he'd never heard anything like it or the volume of it. He made me play it over and over.

Sometimes I walk around Fleet Street when it's empty on Sundays because I secretly want to write for newspapers. Not about news or even music, but about poems and plays. I wonder if they would have me. But I never did any exams.

I also go to the Spiritualist Society for the public readings to see how the different mediums work.

I vividly remember getting into a fight with a skinhead outside a red phone box. An East Asian woman was inside, spilling out a million words in some exotic language quick as she could because she had only a few coins. The skinhead dude was yelling at her to hurry up and he started banging on the door, though I was next in the queue. I said he should leave her alone. He detected I was Irish and yelled at me, "London phone boxes are for London people!" I said, "Well, if you lot had left us a thing of our own in our own countries, we wouldn't need to use your manky phone boxes with their stickers of hooers everywhere, so shut the fuck up." Three of his friends were in the queue, and I think I'd have got my face broken if they hadn't started laughing at him because he'd been out-argued by a girl, and, thank God, for pride-saving alone, he had to pretend he saw the funny side. I got to make my call and they all shook my hand when I was finished, then stood back on the path to make way for me like I was Bishop John McQuaid in Dublin imperially strutting down Grafton Street on Christmas.

A LESSON OR TWO

I HANG AROUND with Fachtna a lot. He has a whole roomful of shelves filled with records. He has more records than anyone I've ever seen. He buys all the records that are on the Jamaican charts from Dub Vendor on Ladbroke Grove. He says every time he moves flats, he takes them all with him. That must be why he doesn't have a wife or a girl-friend — where would she ever put her stuff?

He's been playing me lots of the reggae singles that came out in the last year. I love the Barrington Levy one called "Here I Come," about the guy whose baby's mother makes him take the child because she doesn't wanna be tied down. It's sad, but you wanna leap in the air too, because of the way he uses his voice. When she says she doesn't want the child, he doesn't use words. He just cries out, "Shuddly-wad-dlly-boop-diddly-diddly, w'oh, oh, oh!" and it says all the millions of thoughts and feelings a man would have in that few seconds better than even Oscar Wilde could have.

I'm crazy about the music Fachtna's playing me. Only reggae I ever heard before was "Israelites," "54-46," and "Uptown Top Ranking." But he's played me a guy called Prince Buster. A funny song called "Judge Dread." It's all a crazy courtroom scene, the judge keeps sentencing ev-eryone to four hundred years. And then it has the sweetest but most threatening backing vocals, accompanied by four trumpet notes over and over with drums. And bass and keyboard playing nothing but the chords.

Fachtna took me to see his friend Leroy, who also goes by the name of Lepke. He has a pirate radio station called the Dread Broadcasting Company (the DBC), and he runs a stall on Portobello Road selling reggae records.

Portobello Market runs on Saturdays and Sundays. It's a massive tourist attraction, crowded with people from what must be every country on earth. As they wander by on Saturday afternoons, Leroy blares records from two huge speakers at the front of his stall. Jamaican fashion is to start a record again pretty quickly if it's wonderful. The young people walking by yell "Wheel!" whenever he does it. Then they just keep walking. I love it.

Leroy has a microphone set up on the pavement by the stall. In Jamaica they do a brilliant thing—they release the backing track of records without any vocals so that people can sing along with it themselves, so when you buy the single with the vocal, you also get what's called the "riddim" version as well. Sort of like karaoke, but Jamaican singers even write different lyrics and vocal melodies on the same riddim and all of them are smash hits.

On the first day I went there, Leroy played a riddim or two in the late afternoon. Several young men whose long hair hung down in dreadlocks began wandering over from different directions of the market and commenced nonchalantly browsing through the records and T-shirts. But soon they could be detected inching toward the vicinity of his mike, where they eventually parked themselves, grinding their toes into the ground with shyness and excitement, eyes from floor to mike to each other and back. Much wringing of hands, much rocking, much biting of lips.

As each young man took the mike, it seemed older men with the same type of braids gathered, men who, in their dances, just stepped forward and back, now and again lifting one hand high in the air, as if to warn someone of something. I'd been leaning against the wall behind the stall, but I couldn't make out what the young guys were singing because of their accents. Only four words I'd understood because they were shouted loud whenever they'd come along in the song. Those were *burn, pope, Babylon,* and *blood.* (Also I was pretty sure I'd heard *fire* rhymed with *liar.*)

The realization that all the old guys' arms would raise when those particular words were said made me curious. I sauntered around the side of the stall looking for someone to talk to at the back of the gathering. The voices on the mike kept changing while the riddim did not. A plumpish old fellow was leaning on his bike outside a pub's door lighting the very small end of a spliff that he held with a tweezers. His white hair was so long, he had it wrapped all round his head like a hat but there was enough left over that it hung down the back of his blue shirt.

I put my face in front of his and over the music I said, "Can I ask you something, please?"

He put the spliff behind his back and said, "What if I don't want to hansa?"

I said, "What?"

He said, "I might not want to hansa."

I said, "What are you talking about? I'm not asking you to dance."

He said, "Yuh question, I might not want to hansa hit."

Took ages to understand.

I said, "What's Babylon?"

He laughed.

I said, "Why you laughing?"

He laughed again.

I said, "Why are they saying 'Babylon burn'? And why are they saying the pope must burn, and why are the old guys dancing like that, wagging their fingers in the air?"

He flung his head back, coughing-laughing now. He said, "Ware yuh came from?"

I said, "Ireland."

"Hmm," he said and stared at me in silence out the bottom of his sunglasses for several seconds. Eventually he said, "Hinglan' own dat?"

I said, "What?"

"Do h-England own h-Ireland?"

I said, "No." (There wasn't time to go into it.)

"Well, den," he said, "nobody own God too."

He paused for a moment, looked at me.

"Wat dem teach you inna church inna h-Irelan'? Dem show you Revelayshaan?"

I said, "What?"

He said, "Dem Cyatholic, the pope, an' all dem ting, dem is not a Christian. Dat is why dem didn't infaarm yuh God is comin'. Pope is de devil an' 'im office is de office of de devil. Yuh got yuhself a Bible, daughter?" he asked.

"Yeah, I got a few."

"Well, read Prophet' an' Revelayshaan and check Rasta music all yuh life. Babylon is devil's yard. It will burn because Revelayshaan say it must."

With that he climbed off his bike and wheeled it slowly in the sunset toward Westbourne Grove. I waited awhile to make sure he wasn't looking behind him and then I followed.

The road onto which he turned right and unsaddled was called All Saints. There was a betting shop, a record shop, and a takeout place, outside of which several other old men with lion hairdos were standing around talking in Jamaican accents.

I parked myself on a doorstep not far from them, listening to how they were using words. It was beautiful. I'd never heard English spoken like that. And they weren't like regular old men; they weren't talking about football or politics. They were talking like priests. The long-haired man in the record shop was playing reggae songs real loud, the lyrics all full of Scripture, lines from which got yelled and passionately discussed in the light of his doorway.

I go into the record shop and ask the old man what part of the Bible such-and-such a song he played is from. I have a notebook with me that I take everywhere. I write down what he tells me, then I go home and read the passages. He finds me amusing, I think. He smiles at me so nicely; his face is like a huge sun shining. He says, "What is it today, little daughter?"

Anytime I talk to the old men, they call me "little daughter." If middle-aged men are around, they call me "little sister." They're really kind to me. They never mess about. They're very protective. They ask me if I ate and give me Jamaican patties if I say no. They never mind that I just hang about beside them not saying a whole lot.

INFLAMMABLE MATERIAL

I'M STILL LOOKING at pictures of how to play chords from books. I just throw a capo on my guitar and it changes the keys of the few chord sequences I know. I play as few chords as possible and nothing "posh." I can't do bar chords and I can't play above a whisper. I double-track the guitars on my demos. I have a four-track machine; it's like a tape recorder you can plug a guitar and a mike into. I also have a shiny red mike stand and a black microphone on a lead.

I have two guitars, one twelve-string and one six-string, both Taka-mines. I have an electric keyboard too. All of this equipment and some assorted accoutrements were paid for by Ensign as part of my deal. I have it all set up in my sitting room in Hither Green Lane, but the recording machine is small enough that I can take it places with me.

I play one guitar quietly and record one track, singing the lyrics in my head. Then I play that back and record myself playing the other guitar quietly alongside it so that there's two guitars and it doesn't matter if I'm quiet. When I need to play loud, that way of recording helps too, because layering the guitars disguises how terribly I play. You can turn up and down the levels of your guitars and voice throughout the song and smother it in reverb as you are mixing a final tape of it for yourself.

I bring the tapes into Ensign and make Nigel and Chris listen to them with headphones. They think I have enough songs to start putting a band together so that I can rehearse. Then I'll be ready to actually record when the time comes. They want me to get used to singing my own songs and they want me to write songs with other people too. I'm glad about that because it's my favorite thing when someone else writes the music, given I'm so limited.

Handing me a piece of paper across the table at the Greek restaurant up the road from Ensign's office, Nigel said, "Ali McMordie from Stiff Little Fingers lives in Putney, I want you to go round there on Thursday morning at ten." Jaysus. I nearly passed out because I love Stiff Little Fingers. "You're gonna meet Ali, who plays bass, and a drummer friend of his called John Reynolds. You can write some songs with them."

I went there on the day I was told. As I crossed the road to find the right gate, I saw a man who had just parked a black BMW and was locking it. He had curly hair and was wearing a gray vest that said MIKEY DREAD in green letters. He was carrying two drumsticks. "Are you Sinéad?" he said at the same time I said, "Are you John?"

Ali had a white plaster cast of his girlfriend's arse on his kitchen counter. He brought me and John through to the sitting room to listen to my songs. They really liked "Troy." They asked me what kind of songs I'd like to write with them. I think I just said, "Nothing prissy."

At lunchtime, John and I went out to a café. While we were chatting, I began to see images of a bedroom.

As I mentioned, I sometimes see inside people's houses with my mind. It's not on purpose. It just happens. And there's no big deep or meaningful reason for it.

A little table with small ornaments on it beside the bed. Lace curtains and lavender, a stack of letters on a shelf. The dark curtains drawn.

The images were so strong I asked John if he recognized the room. He said it was his sister Audrey's room. And that she was dying. He was distraught. She was in a lot of pain.

He was minding her far from London but driving to the city every day to work so as to keep his sanity.

With his tight-cut dark curls and his huge blue eyes, John looked like a child. But his body was like a giant's, his hands like massive shovels. He changed the subject. Started telling lewd jokes. Using the C-word more than anyone I'd ever met. I felt we would be bonded for life.

SHAVING MY HEAD

NIGEL IS A SQUARE unto high heaven, as anyone with Nigel for a name is bound to be. He and Chris invited me down to Ensign a few days ago. I had lunch with them at Khan's, and halfway through it Nigel announced he'd like me to stop cutting my hair short and start dressing like a girl. He was disapproving of my recent attempt at a (very short) Mohawk. He said himself and Chris would like me to wear short skirts with boots and perhaps some feminine accessories such as earrings, necklaces, bracelets, and other noisy items one couldn't possibly wear close to a microphone.

When he finished speaking I said to Chris, who had been nodding his head in silent agreement with Nigel's every word, "So, lemme get this straight. He wants me to look like your mistress and the bird he left his wife for?" Silence as I stood up and gathered my keys and ciggies. Chris had such a great face. The huge eyes on him couldn't disguise his admiration for the observation or the mischievousness of finding it so amusing.

When I told Fachtna about events, he said, "I think you should fucking shave your head." I went to the barber's the next day. Greek place by a bathhouse near Ensign and I could call into them straight after the deed was done. I had arranged to swing by on the pretense of having receipts to give Doreen, their lovely secretary, who was a reasonable older blond-haired lady.

The man running the barbershop that day was maybe twenty-six. I was nineteen. He was indeed Greek, mildly plump, short black hair, dark five o'clock shadow. Clearly he'd been left in charge by himself, and despite the fact he had no customers but me, he was in somewhat of a flap.

I slid into his red leather chair and announced, "I want to look like a boy." When it dawned on him exactly what I meant—which because I didn't speak any Greek I made clear by a series of hand gestures that I think might have at first confused him—he went running for the phone on the wall, maybe to call the owner, tears beginning to well up in his eyes.

There was no answer. He was all alone.

"Pleeeeeeeeease dthon'th make me do ith! Pleeeeeeease!" he beseeched, hanging up the phone and walking toward me with his hands held as if in prayer, his tone as soft as if he had given birth to me himself: "Yourh beeeeyoootheefil hayerh."

When he finally got across the room to me, sensing my refusal to be swayed and seeing my eyes so determined, a bloodcurdling terror arose in his mind, and his hand went up instinctively to protect his throat.

"Whath weel your faddthar say?" he uttered with a very sharp intake of breath, and "Whath weel your bruddthar say?" he said as he let it out. Then another sharp breath in and a horrified pause. And then: "Oh maw Gowdth! Whath will your boyfhrendth say? Oh maw Gowdth!" At this, his eyes bulged so with fear that I thought they might pop.

With additional hand gestures, because he didn't speak much Irish, he let me know he really didn't want to risk any males coming round to beat him up. I assured him no one would, though by this stage I was rather considering beating him up myself.

After I'd convinced him that I was the sole author of my own destiny, despite being female, and explained that my father was in Ireland (conveyed by running round the shop with my arms out like a plane and saying, *"Irelandais! Papa est en Irelandais!"*), he agreed to do it. But he made his feelings abundantly clear all the way through. "Ith noth' righth thoo dthoo for gerril."

When he finished I stood up to face him, and one tear rolled down his right cheek.

Me? I loved it. I looked like an alien. Looked like *Star Trek*. Didn't matter what I wore now.

When I walked through Ensign, I got stunned silence from Nigel. Doreen, with her back to him, gave me a silent double thumbs-up with a playful smile. Chris asked me to sit in the car with him later.

"Why've yew dunnit?"

"Because I wanna be me."

"Cawn't yew be yew wiv' 'ayah?"

I said, "It's you who needs hair, you baldy oul fecker, not me. Why don't you let me help you find a doctor?"

THE LION AND THE COBRA

THERE ARE TINY LIGHTS all up and down the massive mixing board, red, yellow, or green, depending how loud you sing. If you get too loud they go red, which means there'll be distortion on tape. Object of my game has been to ride the very finest of fine lines between green and yellow so that it is now less often the case Mr. Happy (the producer) has to worry.

I can tell I'm not gonna have much of a say in mixes when it comes to vocal level, so I need to be sure every word or end of word I sing in a whisper is gonna get heard because the producer just pulls me down to some random level in the mix and leaves me there. The whispered words get lost, and I didn't write them for nothing. So I've made my voice into its own master fader.

I did it by watching the lights on my home-recording device as I sang into the mike with the volume at just above midlevel. I memorized where green finished and let it sink into my body the same way notes do, so the avoidance of yellow is now part of the songs.

You can move around a mike within a certain triangular energy field. The size of each field depends on the type of mike. Some require you to be "on top" of them, as we call it, because the space in which they pick up your voice is so tiny. Others have a larger field and you can throw your head about in order to achieve what you want without the lights going past green. You let your body use the field the same way an actor uses a stage. How far is too far, and how close is too close? You can feel it with your face.

I'm in the middle of recording my first album. Nigel chose the producer, who is a fucking moron and has absolutely no sense of humor, and he needs one, given his terrible beard and how embarrassing he's making my record sound.

Not only have I lost my own sense of humor but I'm a little more drained of the will to live each time the producer plays a song back. I've literally been crying on the inside, smiling on the outside. Because I don't want to hurt anyone's feelings.

The only people I've discussed it with are John Reynolds and Fachtna. John's been here in the studio the whole time because he's the drummer, and we're staying together. So we've often talked about perhaps running away to the other side of Mars in the event the record comes out with our names on it.

In the beginning, in an excellent demonstration of how the term *anal-retentive* might be used in a musical sense, the producer spent hours getting just the bass drum sound right or just the high hat. *Before* recording a note. *Tssh, tssh, tssh* all day long. Who does that? He had the band waiting whole days to play, which meant me waiting late nights to sing, all because he couldn't or wouldn't take a musical shit.

He's had his back to me mostly and he wears a lot of gray. He sits at the center of the sound board in the producer's chair, which is always the biggest of the three swivel chairs in the room. He actually doesn't so much sit at the desk as lean over it with his head in his hands. A position of defeat. He looks like he's planning to fake his own death.

About a fortnight ago Fachtna said that despite the fact I didn't know how to use the studio equipment, I could start fresh and produce my album myself if I want. All I needed to do was tell an engineer what I wanted. He said that's all a producer did anyway.

"But," I said, "what about the hundred thousand pounds the record company has already spent on these recordings? Nigel would have a nervous breakdown, I couldn't upset him like that. If I did that, I may just as well have taken his hundred thousand pounds and thrown it down the toilet." Then Fachtna told me something I hadn't realized, that the hundred thousand pounds was my own money because under the contract, such costs were fully recoupable. Still, I said, I couldn't hurt Nigel's feelings.

But then someone asked me for something on Nigel's behalf, something that wasn't in our contract and that has made me stop caring about either his money or his feelings.

We were in the studio on Friday night recording a cover of the Doors' "Crystal Ship," and I couldn't reach a high note. That had never happened before. I got really mad after the millionth failed attempt and punched the mike. That had never happened before either. As I heard it hit the ground, I thought, *I'm pregnant.* Saturday morning I bought a test from the chemist before I went to the studio. Had to pee in a tiny glass tube that had a small globule of light yellow jelly inside and then sit the tube in a little holder that had a small mirror underneath in which soon a lovely pink circle appeared. Beautiful-looking thing it was too, like a little planet.

I immediately ran and grabbed a cushion from one of the studio reception area's sofas and dashed back to the bathroom to stuff it up my jumper so I could see what I'd look like all fat with a baby; I turned myself this way and that in the mirrors and jumped up and down with excitement. So happy.

John was the father, and when I told him my news the next day at Hammersmith Market, he was shaken.

I fell totally out of love with him and my heart closed. I couldn't have sex with him anymore. I didn't tell him why because I felt guilty. So I told him there must be something wrong with me in the sex department.

117

When I told Nigel, he smiled nicely and said I should go to see Ensign's house doctor to initiate my pregnancy care. I went the next evening.

The doctor told me Nigel had already called him and expressed the wish that he, the doctor, would impress upon me the following, which he, the doctor, said in the following words: "Your record company has spent a hundred thousand pounds recording your album. You owe it to them not to have this baby." Furthermore, he informed me that if I flew while pregnant, my baby would be damaged. And anyway, if I was going to be a musician I ought not have babies because a woman shouldn't leave her baby to go on tour and at the same time a child can't be taken on tour.

I haven't cried so much in years. Nigel can shove his hundred thousand. And his producer. I'm starting again.

Sinéad and her husband, John Reynolds

Sinéad and John Reynolds at home, around 1980

CLOCKS 'N' WOKS

SO I'M AT LEAST a hundred grand in debt starting off, and I earn only five grand a year. If this record doesn't make that money back and more, because it's the second time it's been recorded, I will never be financially independent of people with penises. Speaking of which, I'm also nearly as pregnant as a person can be. Baby is rolling around nicely and I'm beside myself with excitement. I hope it's been okay in there when I've been recording vocals. Some of the songs are nothin' but a load of yelling.

I got thrown out of an Italian café in Charing Cross last week by the old lady running the place because I had on, cut short so that my bump was exposed, a white T-shirt on which was printed ALWAYS USE A CON-DOM. She wasn't seeing the funny side.

I'm staying in an old-fashioned bed-and-breakfast place in Putney. I'll be staying there for the next three weeks while we mix the album. It's a red-brick family-looking house with, thank God, only one flight of stairs. The street is a family-looking street. The houses are all family-looking. Cream linen handkerchiefs with tiny lilies embroidered in each corner are folded in triangles on my bedside cabinets. A glass jug with a belly like mine sits in vain hope, full of water on the shelf by the telly. I haven't touched it.

I've enjoyed waddling my fat self along the white fences and overgrown trees of the street to the studio for the past few days. All in all, it's a lot nicer than where we stayed when we were recording, the Kypriana Hotel. Aptly named because in Dublin a hideous dump is slangily called a "kip."

There were actually fleas. John Reynolds and I endured every manner of them and their tiny teeth in the nights. But we did so gladly, because we were acutely aware that our being there meant we had by some miracle become ex-thieves and now had the chance of earning a legitimate living. If we hadn't been in the music business we'd be stealing a lot of stuff together and ending up in separate jails.

When John and I first met, the back of his car was full of clocks and woks. He and his mate had broken into some vast warehouse; it was coming up to Christmas and they had no money. They were selling some of the clocks and woks they'd stolen and giving others to the females in their lives as Christmas presents. John's mother got a clock *and* a wok. The less revered females got one or the other.

The thing I'm gonna remember most about making our record is when I met John Keogh. He was lying on the floor outside the studio toilet hugging himself because he'd just jacked up a load of smack. "'Ullo, Shine-eyed," he slurred in his East London accent and then giggled at himself as his eyes rolled up into the back of his head. Just as I lifted my foot to step over him he said, "Daan' warry, I wown' look ap y' skuh'."

He is the bass player with Max, and we were recording their song "Just Call Me Joe."

He has thick black eyelashes long as spider legs. His eyes are real pale yellow-green. Look like dandelion clocks. Whenever he's been at my place, his eyes have spun round on his face like the snake's in *The Jungle Book* because he's always on the class A drugs. But he's not a snaky person; he's an innocent. That's why he can't bear the world.

He leans against my door. Says he has no sisters, so he likes talking to me. He looks at me like he's impressed, like a child in awe. I asked him why. He said he should never have been asked to be a grown-up and I should never have been asked to be a child. He's impressed that anyone would want to be a grown-up.

His smile makes people smile because he slightly cry-laughs. He tries to hide that he's so beautiful because he gets beaten up for it round his neighborhood. He'll turn his face away or look down. He dresses scruffy and has zits and his teeth are gray from smack and yellow from everything else. But he does employ the smile when the smack has closed his eyes. He's very clever. It's always for other people's benefit, never his own. He wants us not to worry about him. He wants us to think he's okay. But he isn't okay. Eventually he falls asleep in the bath.

For the mixing, it's been just me and the engineer and the tape ops. They get the shitty jobs, mostly. Running round making endless cups of tea and coffee for musicians and producers, having to be in before everyone else and be last to leave. Having to go out to the shops for sandwiches or any other fancies of the contingent. They're nerds, but strictly in the sense that Superman is a nerd. And from observing them, I've come to realize that if not for nerds, no records would ever be made. There'd just be a load of stoned musicians and coked-up record executives, the latter too busy pleading not guilty to aggravated sexual harassment on the grounds of being over-coked, and getting away with it, to be of any service in the recording process.

No other type of man is capable of performing the task from which a tape op takes his name. This man can do something no other man would dare risk. The bosses in the studio situation make him do it because among all of them, he has the least to lose. But the fact that he can do it makes him king over all.

He can splice the tape to make an edit.

So if the first half of the song went along nicely but the second half was shite, and it was the other way round on the previous take, he can make a slice with a Wilkinson Sword razor blade across the tape just be-

123

fore it all went wrong and make a slice in the previous tape just before it all went right and stitch them together with special adhesive so that the whole song is right and you don't have to record all over again.

He does it by getting the producer to play the track and then, once the desired place of edit has been established, the track is put into slow-motion playback around that area. As these playbacks are happening, the tape op is eyeing the tape as it rolls round the two reels. Eventually he will gently take hold of the sides of both reels and turn them this way and that until the song gets so slow and the vocal so deep that it sounds like a horror movie. He'll keep turning the tapes until he finds the shortest of breaths in the music and observe where it is on the tape. Only when his eye can recognize it will he remove his hands, at which point he pulls a four-inch section of the tape from between the two reels down onto a little steel bridge that looks like a leprechaun's train tracks and makes a vertical line with tailor's chalk.

He has one slice in which to get it right. Disaster will result if he messes it up. A lot of money (and a lot of artistic temperament) is in the room. Knuckles are desperately held between teeth. Everyone silent as a ghost for the one and a half minutes it takes for the cut to be made, the adhesive applied, and the tape played back. Because he is lord of all, it never goes wrong; it is pristine on the first shot. He gets to rest awhile with his feet on the cream leather puff, having coffee and biscuits brought to him for a change by whoever the bosses are. He is cosmetic surgeon to the stars.

MY BOY LOLLIPOP,
JULY 1987

JAKE WENT BLUE in his little blanket from toe to head in my room on me, so I got the nurse and she grabbed him and ran off down the corridor; she wouldn't let me come. I was frantic. An older nurse was passing by my door, and out the window behind her I could see the opposite wing of the hospital, the part where people go to die. I took her by the arm and pleaded, "My baby went blue and they've taken him —he's not going to die, is he?"

"I hope not," she replied and kept walking.

Jaysus. That would never happen in Ireland. Someone would hold your hand. But I'm at John Radcliffe Hospital in Oxford. I'm twenty years old, like. This is my first baby. I've never been so frightened in my life.

That night of his birth, I had a terrible dream that the doctor came into the room with the child all wrapped in a blanket and he gave the child to me, but as I put the child up on my shoulder, he fell out of the blanket and onto the floor and his little forehead broke like a teacup. I hoped that that was not a bad omen for my parenting skills.

He's back now, thanks be to God. They put him in an incubator for an hour. He's a little early and he's only six pounds, six ounces. I'm kind of tiny, so he is too. That's what the nurse said.

Also, after he came out, I think they left him on me too long without wrapping him up. They were so busy faffing with the placenta, he froze his little butt off. It's hot inside a body, so it stands to reason it's freezing when you come out. Nothing in the books warned me, so I didn't have a blanket. And the birth room didn't have one. He wasn't wrapped up for a good half an hour.

A friend of John's told me to drink a load of castor oil as soon as I went into labor. I don't know why I took her advice. She said it would make the birth easier. But then, she's the one who, nine months previously, told me the fourteenth day of your cycle is the only day you *can't* get pregnant. She never told me if I drank castor oil I'd shit for Ireland and the birth would be so quick there'd be no time for drugs.

There was a poor little student nurse in a blue uniform on that night. She couldn't have been more than eighteen. It was really late. She had to keep giving me little gray papier-mâché bowls to shit in, and then she had to carry them away when they were full. I must have filled about twenty of them. The blackest-lookin' shit I've ever seen in my life, apart from the one my lovely little son did about half an hour after he was born. That was like tar toothpaste. Am thus very impressed with him so far. But also because he's really cute and red and hairy. He's exactly like a baby monkey.

Jake was born at four minutes to four a.m. Long, rough night. John went home to get some sleep after showering the blood off me at about five a.m., a task magnanimously assigned to him by the midwife as though it were the greatest honor one could bestow upon a man who's spent the night watching his woman give birth in and all over his poshest white dinner shirt (word to the wise: Never lend a full-term pregnant woman an item of clothing you want back).

He's not too happy about the haircut I gave him the night before last, so he had fun splattering me against the tiles with cold water instead of warm. My defense is that he asked me to do it, and anyone who puts someone with my haircut in charge of his own deserves what he gets. I sheared the sides rather badly and I don't know how to blend. He nearly cried when he saw it.

But I think I've made up for it 'cause he loves his little baby, and he's said I can wear his blue and white nightshirt. And his mum is gonna come down from Liverpool the day after tomorrow to see her first grandchild. She's lovely, John's mum. I love her. She's from Yorkshire and she's as bold as a little child. Eating sweets when she's diabetic. Betty is her name. It really suits her, 'cause she has big brown Betty Boop eyes.

She has a crazy dog, though. No way am I bringing Jake to her house. The postmen keep quitting. She's had her garage converted into a front room, all pretty and flowery. What was the garage door is now a huge window. Stupid dog keeps launching himself through it when anyone passes the gate. It's a Doberman. I hate it. It pinned me against the wall for ages the second I met Betty. *Sooo* embarrassing.

Betty's so nice to John. She just adores him. She only pretend-scolds him. He farts out loud all the time around her and they crack up laughing. John's sister Maria is the same. Maria has tons of tattoos but Betty doesn't know.

I wish I were Betty's daughter. Or one of the kids she raised. She's so kind and gentle. Her voice is so loving and warm. It goes up and down like a mother's voice should. Her boys come to visit her still. They're men now, like John. They adore her; she loved them onto the straight and narrow. They have jobs because of her. And girlfriends and all.

One of her sons told his girlfriend he was going round the corner for cigarettes and didn't come back for two years. Then they got married. He's really funny. He's gonna be a lovely dad.

I want to make clear I don't blame John (or my dad, for that matter) for being concerned about me having a baby. There were many reasons to be concerned. And I know they meant the very best for me.

I don't believe that in the case of the record company, though. Their only expressed concern was money, whereas John and my father were worried about my youth. Valid concerns based on love, in other words.

John really deserves his own chapter in this book because he's like my brother and my best friend in this world. I have known him since I was eighteen and he was twenty-eight. And that's a long set of years. He has always been there for me as a friend even when I've been wrong. He has always been my rock. And has always taken care of me.

I've had the absolute funniest times of my life with John and I've never laughed so much with any other human being. Nor farted out loud as much. John is a legendary farter-out-loud. And it's catching.

Today, his studio is at the very top of the home he shares with Fiona, his amazing wife, and their two daughters, Jesse and Ruby.

All manner of artists have worked and stayed there. From Seun Kuti to Robert Plant to the Indigo Girls to myself to Damien Dempsey—basically, anyone you can think of. Because John is an utter musical midwife. He is able (sometimes by farting out loud) to make people feel so comfortable that they can fully be themselves in a way they couldn't in any other studio. He always gets the very best out of any performer.

John has two bullmastiff dogs and loves them like they are his children. He is an amazing father and Fiona's an amazing mother. I've never once heard a raised voice in their house that wasn't singing.

He has been and still is an incredible father to Jake. And thank God, Jake is the spit of him, as we say in Ireland. They are so alike.

I couldn't find words to describe how much I love John and how much he means to me. He is my family. And I wouldn't have sung nearly anything well if not for the fact I was comfortable enough with him to be recording there in my pajamas and slippers, him making me cry-laugh with farts emitted in time to backing tracks . . .

I'd be lost without John in my life. I'd be nothing without the companionship and creativity and brotherhood and laughter and emotional support he has given me. He is the very anchor of my life. There just are not words. But the catalog of music we have made together over the course of the last thirty-five years says it all and is the legacy of our bond. A beautiful dance through life we have had together. And still have. And always will have.

THE WAY YOUNG LOVERS DO

WHEN JOHN WENT to pick Betty up at the station, I gave Jake his first bath. Poor creature roared crying; it was terrible. He was red all over from upset. He's so little. Betty fell in love. She's so cool. She gave him a statue of a cute fat rabbit with green trousers on and a yellow shirt and a big smile.

Having Jake was also somewhat discombobulating. One day about a week after Jake was born, me and John went out in the car and didn't remember we had a baby until we were about a hundred feet down the road. Nearly had a heart attack when we realized. Screeched the car round and went back home for him.

Another night I had a terrible nightmare that I left Jake with my mother to mind him while I went shopping. Never had such a frightening dream in my life. Woke up sweating and feeling for Jake in the low light to make sure it wasn't true.

Babies don't actually smile at you for six weeks, and when Jakey smiles, it's the most beautiful gummy thing I've ever seen. His whole face and eyes light up. The first time he did it, he was lying on his little belly in my bed.

Apart from John Reynolds, the person during that time who unequivocally supported my desire to be both a touring musician and a mother was Fachtna, my manager. He was the only one saying I *could* be a good mother and that he'd make sure there was always help. I'd known him for two years, and now he'd become my hero.

Three months after Jake was born and my album was about to come out, reviews were in the papers, and our promo trips were kicking off.

I'm twenty and in Blooms Hotel in Dublin. As I carry a tray of coffee to where Joe Jackson from *Hot Press* is sitting in the bar waiting to interview me, my arms and legs are shaking. We've flown in from London to promote *The Lion and the Cobra*. I don't know who these people I'm meeting are meeting, but it isn't me.

We're in the American Hotel in Amsterdam and I'm in a room talking to ten people a day, one after the other, all of them with microphones and notepads in their hands. With cameras and flashing white lights. Will I stand this way or that?

I don't even know what town we're in. I don't care what's for lunch. I don't care why I made a record. I don't even know what planet I'm on.

Whatever Fachtna thinks is a good idea is a good idea. What he loves, I love. What he hates, I try to hate. All I want to do is keep impressing him. I say whatever I imagine will impress him. I become whatever I imagine will impress him.

Sometimes I think I'm more like him than me.

London, circa 1989. New look, new career.

KATE GARNER

THERE IS A LIGHT AND IT NEVER GOES OUT, 1987

I AM ON TOUR in freezing England, supporting INXS. Right after I had agreed to tour with them, David Bowie asked me to support his band. It was a disappointment that I couldn't accept but it's brilliant that he asked me nonetheless. Mike Joyce and Andy Rourke, from the Smiths, are in my band. Andy is the funniest person I've ever met in my life. I love him.

Andy and his brothers would be on acid when the parish priest came round for tea with them and their father. The boys had to try to act normal round the table and not be crying-laughing. That's one reason I love Andy—he cry-laughs. Crying-laughing is the greatest feeling ever and the funniest thing to watch. Him and Mike are really funny together. They make each other roll around on the floor. I love Mike too. They've made me love Manchester people. Dead straight. No bullshit. No un-frank conversation. Also, they treat me like a boy, which makes me a happy girl.

Among musicians, there really doesn't exist the attitude toward females that exists among the suits of the music industry (and that exists generally in Ireland). So while I'm with musicians and road crew, it's good to be a girl. It's mostly guys I'm around, and they treat me like a guy, so I'm learning real well how to be like a guy.

You're safer being a traveling musician if you feel like you're a guy.

Not safe as in "safe from people" but safe from life on the road being rough and from the fact you're a female uncommon to what is outlined as natural. You're acting like you have the same freedoms as men. That's gonna be hard for you to manage. A woman's place is in the home. Not on Highway 66. Especially if she is a mother as I am. You're gonna be doing your own head in for the rest of your life every time you go to work if you don't keep telling yourself you're a man.

It's so lovely when people like Andy or Mike or John Reynolds or John Keogh or John Maybury's gang don't treat me any differently because I'm a girl. Except in nice ways, like when Maybury, the video director, gets someone to put makeup on me and keeps telling me I'm pretty. He's gay as Christmas so it's even nicer than when a straight man says it because straight men all say it to get laid. John Maybury and all his friends say it because they love girls. They make me feel really nice about being a girl. But I like to look like a boy. They've never blinked an eye about it. No one does. Except poor Nigel Grainge.

I like to look like John Maybury's friend Alan, basically. He's so handsome, with a crew cut, and he has a soft, lovely voice. His eyes always brim full of gentleness when he looks at absolutely anyone. His whole heart is in his eyes at all times. He doesn't have a temper and he isn't afraid of people. I wish I were like him. I have a temper, and I'm afraid of most people.

Maybury, not long before, had pulled off an amazing musical/promotional coup. It's 1987, and there's full war in Northern Ireland, but despite this, Maybury and his crazy lighting man managed to carry pounds and pounds of napalm from Heathrow through Dublin airport, unobserved at either end, to use in a video shoot. We rigged up the Hellfire Club, an infamous eighteenth-century ruin on a hill overlooking Dublin. Must have blown it up five times. It's a national monument. We didn't even ask permission. The dude who rigged it was an army expert. Nothing fell off or over. We left the structure intact.

It was for the video of my first single, "Troy." We shot the first part in a freezing-cold studio in East London. John had all his friends working on the video. They shaved my head completely bald with a bunch of Bics. Then they covered me from head to chest in pure gold leaf, like that James Bond girl, and sat me to sing in a circle of fire. I was going round and round all day on a little train track, and John told me to keep "finding the camera." I look like a very pissed-off alien whose breath sets fire to stuff.

Anyway, back to INXS. I met Michael Hutchence in the Dublin airport when we were all checking in for the first date of the tour. He was really nice to me. He's like a big-brother type. He's protective. Not flirty or anything. He isn't around much but when I've hung out with him there's been lots of people everywhere and he always watches out for me very quietly, no matter if he's chatting someone up across the room on some sofa or talking to friends or whatever. He makes sure some idiot doesn't talk me into bed or bore me to death with music-industry talk. I like him. He doesn't say a lot with words. He says it with looks. He's like some kind of American Indian.

During the tour, me and Andy Rourke got beaten up in Liverpool by the bouncer of our hotel's basement disco. Big hairy monster. Looked like he served in Belfast for the Brits. The mustache on him and all, so reminiscent.

He didn't like my Doc Martens. Fair enough. They have steel toecaps sticking out; as is the fashion, I have sliced the leather to reveal them. And he didn't like my shaved head. Andy and I went upstairs and I changed shoes but when we get back down, I still had a shaved head, and we'd been giggling.

Andy's face looked cheeky at the ticket box. He'd got the nervous giggles. Monster Man decided we were trouble and punched him. Then he ran after us into the lift and beat the shit out of the two of us. One of his friends came and dragged me out of the lift by my shirt neck and up some stairs, *bump-bump* all the way, while Monster Man did the same to

Andy. We got dumped into the street. The two of us were in bits. I lost it. We went back up to our rooms and I jumped all round the bedroom for an hour threatening to go down and kill him. Poor Fachtna had to wait for me to fall asleep to make sure I didn't, piling chairs up at the door to keep Monster Man out and me in.

There's a very good reason that God made the word *touring* rhyme with the word *whoring*. In fact, most of what I can remember about touring, especially in my younger days when I was doing huge U.S. and European tours to support my albums, was it was nothing but sex. That's all any of us had on our minds. We did the gigs. It was a pleasant interlude between doing the gigs. While we weren't busy breaking hearts, myself and the other ladies in my band would often travel on the gentlemen's crew bus. Crazy, because you just don't do that in America, certainly not without your tour manager. All those buses rocked from side to side all down the highways.

I guess we did end up breaking some hearts, though, because most of the crew were married or had girlfriends and we wouldn't continue our relationships. At the end of the tour, we dumped them like a bunch of hot snots, which was quite cruel because we did like them. It was foolish of them because we were just being sluts. As I said, we liked them, we did. They were nice guys, but you know, they had girlfriends, and as we say in the music business, on tour doesn't count. That's the attitude we had.

The tour I best remember was actually for my second album, *I Do Not Want What I Haven't Got*. At this stage I had a new manager, Steve Fargnoli, who had been Prince's manager. And because "Nothing Compares 2 U" on the album had been number one, it was suddenly a whole other world for me on tour.

There was a stylist, lighting guys; there was a *production*, all kinds of pomp and ceremony. I found it hard to get used to because I had a lot of stage fright and I felt like a total impostor. I couldn't understand why anybody liked my songs or why anybody clapped or thought they were good. I really had no self-esteem when it came to songs or anything else.

And I'd be playing these festivals or carnivals and there'd be people screaming nearby on roller coasters, people screaming in terror, and I'd be singing soothing songs to the audience. It was just the weirdest thing — triggering, actually. I also got into the habit of singing with my eyes closed, which really upset my manager. I came to prefer it for a number of reasons, including the fact that if you made eye contact with someone's boyfriend, you got scared his girl was going to beat you up afterward, especially if you were doing a romantic song. Between the thrill-ride screams and the fear of jealous rage, I developed the ability to just close my eyes while performing and go into my own world.

Touring was ultimately a very lonely thing. There were a lot of people around me, people I loved, even, but no one could see me and I couldn't see myself reflected in anyone anymore. Suddenly there was no one around me who I'd known before I became very famous. I had cut myself off from my family. Not their fault — mine.

I found the touring experience of sitting around in hotel rooms all day quite lonely. And the promo thing? I got in trouble every time I opened my mouth. People would ask me a question; I'd answer it; I'd be in trouble. I just couldn't be accepted as a good person. It was hurtful. Everybody was starting to treat me like I was a crazy person too.

You're probably not aware of the fact that no matter whether you're the queen of England or Barbra Streisand or Bob Dylan or anyone else, you may not take a shit on a tour bus. There will be a sign on the door that says NO SOLIDS. This makes for very interesting touring.

I would love to put together a toilet book, if you will, called *No Solids*. I would like to write to Mariah Carey and Barbra Streisand and even the queen of England and get them to send me their stories. It would be especially funny if it was only very huge female stars, like Céline Dion.

My own stories about trying to take poops are not very funny. They're kind of disturbing, actually, so I'm not going to bother. Well, once I got stuck in a field in France, and I couldn't see anything past my face. I was on tour with Sly and Robbie, and the bus is so close to me that I can't take a shit because I am embarrassed, but then it won't come, and the next thing you know I'm afraid they're all going to get out of the bus so I can't take the shit, and I'm stuck there, literally.

Eventually somebody does get out of the bus, which makes me so scared that I take the shit. But I'm sure other people have funnier stories than me because when you're on a tour bus with fourteen people, the fact that nobody can take a shit on the bus means you got to stop fourteen times and different times of the day or night.

GOOD NEWS, BAD NEWS,
ET CETERA

INSIDE ME, WHILE FACHTNA spoke each word on the phone — "You've been nominated for a Grammy" — I saw my life roll up as if it were a blanket and vanish. Quick as a flash, like I was a dying person. I've never told anyone. I'm like Stevie Nicks. She keeps her visions to herself.

The nomination for *Lion and the Cobra* in 1989 was career-changing. Of course, my next nomination, a couple years later for *I Do Not Want What I Haven't Got*, brought me an inordinate amount of satisfaction on a different level. That's because it hadn't been so long before that Nigel called to say he didn't want to release that album. His exact words were "It's too personal; it's like reading someone's diaries. It will end up like Terence Trent D'Arby's second album, gathering dust in a warehouse."

He'd been privy to the bloody songs for months before recording began, and the thing was already mastered. I wondered what on earth he was on. I think he just enjoyed being piggish.

I reminded him that my contract gave me creative control, which meant the album was coming out whether he liked it or not.

The man is such an (oxy)moron. How can a song be too personal? I imagined slapping him lightly about the temples with a large raw fish. That's the only thing to do to stupid people.

Within months, *I Do Not Want What I Haven't Got* is number one all over the planet, and Nigel hasn't had to so much as lift a phone to make millions for himself. I'm pleased for him. Because an idiot can never get laid if he isn't stinking rich.

One of the factors contributing to my album's success began in a Paris cemetery. At Père Lachaise, a queen-size bed is carved in snow-white marble. There a young woman lies, wearing a beautiful buttoned nightdress, smiling at her baby, blankets pulled up around them, baby smiling back. Every detail, down to the stitches in the sheets and blankets, perfect. Every smile line under the woman's eyes. Even her hair on her pillow.

I walked around there most of the day in an extraordinarily expensive coat I wished I could keep. Gerry Stafford, the stylist, told me Père Lachaise even had its own sewage system. I must admit I was slightly freaked at the idea of the dead getting up to take a dump and then shuffling back into their tombs. Also, what do they wipe with?

Note to self: Never, ever go to a graveyard again.

We were making the video for "Nothing Compares 2 U." We'd already shot most of the video in London a few days ago, maybe three setups. In one, a close-up, I just sang the song along with the track, sitting in a chair wearing a black polo neck. But in the part where it says "All the flowers that you planted, Mama, in the backyard, all died when you went away," I cried for like twenty seconds.

I think that means I wasted their time. I did manage to get my act together and keep singing. But I think it's unusable. So it's good we're shooting all this stuff in Paris. I feel bad I wasted everyone's time and money, though.

John Maybury, who again directed my video, thought I was crying because me and Fachtna had recently parted ways. But I'm happy about that now. It's better for everyone.

I was crying about my mother being dead. I'm still really messed up about it, even though I'm twenty-four. A little embarrassing. But there you go. I'm a girl.

• • •

In the showbiz parts of Los Angeles, the white walls have beautiful dark pink flowers. The Mexicans live elsewhere. So do the African-Americans. The only time you see those people, they're cleaning someone's house.

In the New York office of my record company, the color of the employees' skin is darkest in the basement, which is the mail room. Their skins get lighter as the floors go up. As do the stations the employees have their radios tuned to. Two floors from the top, "no females" becomes the scenario also. Unless they're in secretarial roles.

The bosses didn't like the album-cover shot for *Lion and the Cobra*, so we had to have a different one for America, but from the same series. They felt I looked "angry" on the European one. I look like I'm screaming. In fact, I was singing. The very clever photographer made me sing along to my record, which he'd cranked up real loud. So it's just what I look like when I'm singing. But the bosses liked the "demure" look of the one where I'm looking at the floor and my mouth is shut. Apparently females seeming angry doesn't "shift units." And they're already handicapped by my hair.

The people who run the music industry aren't punk at all. They're a bunch of frightened people. But frightened of the wrong thing— namely, music. Hence in 1991, there was a rap category at the Grammys, but they didn't televise the award. So there was a boycott amongst the rap community. Hence I once had Public Enemy's logo shaved and dyed onto the side of my head so it would be seen on telly all around the world.

Showbiz just got real interesting. The kids are beginning to revolt (and no one has been revolting since John Lennon died).

Rap is the hugest thing in America. All you see are teenagers (referred to as "kids" by the establishment) sitting on steps with enormous boom boxes, blaring Public Enemy or KRS-One so loud that the bass would nearly make you defecate or lugging the boom boxes round the streets on their shoulders like they're walking the stations of the cross.

Similar to Christ's, rap's mission is self-esteem for those "previously deemed shit." So it's as dangerous as Christ's. Because a lot of kids of all manner are listening, and no one in the industry wants their top floors threatened by either the wrong skin color or the wrong mindset—that is, anyone who cares about truth.

Kids are the market, but you have to keep them believing they're worth less than the stars or they won't think they need what stars are selling.

Wait till you see. When showbiz execs realize they can't kill rap, they will hijack it. They'll make millionaires of impostor rappers who say things like "You can't be like me."

FUNNY HOW TIME
SLIPS AWAY

I ACTUALLY ATTENDED the Grammys for the 1989 show when I'd been nominated for Best Female Rock Vocal, and I performed "Mandinka."

All through the dress rehearsal, I was anxious because the previous day, when we'd arrived in LA, I had gone into one of those little houses on Sunset Boulevard that have a flashing sign in the window saying PSYCHIC.

An ancient Indian woman, plump and wearing a purple and orange sari, emerged from behind a red curtain. "Sit down," she said to me and pointed to a battered pale green armchair to her left. She went away for a few minutes, came back, and plonked herself in its match opposite me.

We chatted for about ten minutes. Nothing in particular came up, other than I told her my mother was dead and that I wanted to know if she was okay wherever she was. She told me, "That's not what I do. You need a medium."

Then she said, "Let me see your palm," and I gave her my right hand. She said, "I see dark spirits around you."

Big gulp on my part. "Why are they there? How do I get rid of them?"

"They are there because you are sad," she said. "You must have a bath and fill a plastic bottle with the water afterward."

And she continued: "For each of your years on earth, you must strap a

143

At the Grammys with Al Green and BP Fallon

BP FALLON

hundred-dollar bill to the bottle with elastic and give it to me. That is the cure."

I ran back to the hotel and told Fachtna, "I need two thousand dollars ASAP." He wouldn't give it to me. He wouldn't ask the record company for it. He said I was being had, that the woman was a trickster. I could see he was right, but she'd scared me, so I plagued him all night and morning about it. I wanted to do it anyway. We were still annoyed with each other when it was time to go to the dress rehearsal. We're often annoyed with each other.

We sat in the middle of the third row during rehearsal as Sarah Vaughan coughed her way through the song "So Many Stars." I was impressed. That was her warm-up. After she'd coughed and sung it three times, her voice was perfect. Clear, smokeless, and beautiful.

Dizzy Gillespie's cheeks blew out like balloons as he rehearsed. I wanted to kiss them, he looked so cute.

Al Green wore a shirt made from gold. It looked like a ton of tiny chains all stitched together. Someone introduced us to him. He smelled amazing. Like perfume, not aftershave. I joked that I should ask him if he would marry us, since he's a minister. But I don't think a marriage between two such grumpy people as us would be much fun.

I met Anita Baker. She was rehearsing too, wearing a gorgeous black and gold dress. I love her. She's so beautiful. She was holding a long-stemmed red rose. She gave it to me. She said she liked "Mandinka." She said, "Your voice is cavernous."

When I got back to my hotel room after the rehearsal, a massive arrangement of pink balloons with balloons inside them was tied to a chair. I'd never seen such a thing. The record company had sent them.

For the show, I wore a short top and a pair of jeans. I stuck the arms of Jake's sleep suit through the belt loops at the back so that it hung down my arse. Later, when I got home to Ireland, I put it on my mother's grave. It's still there, though much more frail. It is sunken into the mud and rocks. It used to be blue and white. Now it's yellow, like someone soaked it in chamomile tea.

My older brother was angry that I put it there. He found it an upsetting image. He thought it a messed-up thing to do. But I meant it as a souvenir for her from the Grammys. Because all the time I was there, I was thinking how she would have loved to be there too. And she was never gonna meet her grandson. I wanted to give her something of him.

A visit to Hollywood
BP FALLON

PAPER ROSES

MY SECOND GRAMMY NOMINATIONS came in 1991. It was very different from my initial honors, because I didn't go. And I rejected the award I won for Best Alternative Music Performance. To the great consternation of many, I refused *all* the awards I was personally offered for my second album. Because I knew after how I'd spent the year being treated by the industry and media that I wasn't getting awards because of anything I stood for. Rather, I was getting awards because I'd "shifted a lot of units"—sold a lot of records. Commercial success outranked artistic merit. I made a lot of money for a lot of men who couldn't actually have cared less what the songs were about. And in fact would prefer I told no one.

I make plain as I'm refusing awards and award shows that I am doing so in order to draw attention to the issue of child abuse. And that I'm a punk, not a pop star. And that awards make some people feel more than and some people feel less than. And that music shouldn't be such a competition.

There is outrage at me throughout the industry. In England, the Brit Awards are hosted by Jonathan King, a hugely popular television DJ. For some reason he spends ten minutes viciously attacking me for my stance. It's quite baffling. His eyes are bulging and his mouth is foaming, he's so angry. How dare the little Irish upstart associate music with child abuse?

(Not too many years later when he's convicted and jailed for repeated acts of pedophilia, his rage makes sense.)

In America I'm bullied very badly by certain men on the night I skipped the Grammys. In fact, I'm even spiked. At a watching party in Eddie Murphy's house. Which scares the shit out of me.

I leave LA three days later and go back to England. I give my LA house to the Red Cross. I don't want anything to do with the trappings of so-called success anymore.

Prince and his half brother Duane

SHEVITI ADONAI L'NEGDI TAMID

I TRIED TO GET lessons in Jewish ways of understanding the Scriptures but no one would take me because I'm not Jewish. Nor have I yet found myself that (much-fantasized-about) handsome rabbi who wants to marry me so I have to become Jewish because I truly love him. The closest I've been able to get is kabbalah classes with a very kind teacher named Z'ev Ben Shimon Halevi in a small school in gorgeous Regent's Park.

Happened to be I had a class both myself and the teacher sadly knew would be my last a few days after I'd heard that "Nothing Compares 2 U" and *I Do Not Want What I Haven't Got* had gone to number one in America. Appropriately, the moment I'd heard, I was sitting on a toilet (I can't remember whose) with the door open as usual (for the purposes of easy chat). Whoever it was who told me got cross with me because I didn't take the news happily. Instead I cried like a child before the gates of hell.

That night I dreamed I was a golden orchestra triangle with arms and legs and a face just making my way through Regent's Park along old, dusty paths. People were running up, taking pieces of my body. I had to rush home, get an old raincoat, and cover myself up wherever I went. If people knew I was made of gold, someday there'd be none of me left.

Soon as I arrived for my last lesson, the kabbalah teacher spun me out the classroom door by my elbow, took me into the corridor, and whispered loudly in my ear, "You know fame is a curse and the devil is a gentleman?"

I nodded in the affirmative, and he swung me back in, saying, "Don't forget to leave the party before they all get drunk and start fighting."

Nine months later my tour has finished and I've rented a house in Los Angeles because my manager said I couldn't go home until after the MTV awards. Spanish-looking house halfway up a hill. Beautiful old white stucco on the outside. Even a tiny cross at the front door, just like Ireland. I can see the Hollywood sign way off to my left when I'm on my patio. Sometimes there are deer meandering about amid the trees to my right.

One whole wall of the downstairs sitting room is a glass window facing Los Angeles. At night, it's like a black frame around the lights of living hell. Every time the dusk comes, I get anxious.

I had my bedroom painted purple. I thought, *What the hell, you can have a purple bedroom in America, that's the whole point.* In Ireland you'd never have a purple bedroom unless you were a hooer. And since in Ireland sex is a sin, you can't be a hooer because you wouldn't have any customers. So no one has ever had a purple bedroom, apart from Archbishop John Charles McQuaid.

As I'm figuring out what to wear one midweek morning, the phone rings in my room. An effeminate but irritated male voice asks, "Is that Shine-head O'Kahn-er?"

I say, "No, this is Sinéad O'Connor," just to wind him up. Then I ask him who he is.

He says he's Prince.

Says he wants to send a car down for me later, and let's hang out.

I met him in a club when *Lion and the Cobra* came out, but we never really talked. We were just getting off on the tunes the DJ was playing, Sly Stone and such.

We haven't spoken since. He didn't have anything to do with my recording of "Nothing Compares 2 U." His call to my purple bedroom is the first time we've been in contact since 1988.

I'm twenty-three. When I tell my friends about Prince's call, they get romantic ideas. We all thought maybe me and him would fall in love.

At the very least, we imagined me and him would get on well, because the lovely Steve Fargnoli (who had become my manager) had previously managed him and had introduced us.

We thought: *He must be wanting to celebrate the song doing so well! There'll be cake! Princes always have cake!*

I was thrice wrong, and my poor girlfriends went from agape to aghast when I later told them what went down.

At nine p.m., from the darkness of my bedroom window, I see the long black limousine slink to a silent stop at my gate. I imagine I'm in a spy movie about to be driven to a secret location where I'm gonna be given my next mission.

The stereotypical driver with suit and hat is behind the wheel. I'm a yapper, so on the way I ask him all about Prince and what the house is like et cetera. He never says one word, just looks at me scared every now and then in the rearview mirror as if I've asked him for directions to Dracula's castle. Very strange. Usually drivers like to chat as much as girls do.

We drive a long time before winding our way up a black-dark hill, at the top of which appears a large house, very dimly lit. We pull into its driveway. The front door is to my right. It seems we're in a courtyard, beyond which, facing me about two hundred feet away, I discern some outbuildings.

I get out of the car and the driver gestures with his head to say I can go ring the doorbell by myself. This I do. I wait several moments and nothing happens. I ring again and still nothing. I turn round to ask the driver's opinion as to what I ought to do, but he and the limousine have vanished.

Just as I'm realizing I have no idea where I am or how to get home in the event no one is in and that the road is so dark I won't be able to see farther than my eyelashes, the door opens slowly with a creak.

I'm thinking the person behind it is gonna say, "You rang?" like in the movies and be named Igor. Turns out his name is not Igor. But I don't find that out until later.

Seems like nobody speaks around here; they just use movements of the head. He indicates I'm to step inside and follow him. This I do, observing in his deportment a definite air of "Master, Master," though he's not quite dragging one leg. His chin is down, his arms are straight by his sides, his shoulders are attempting to protect his heart.

Through two enormous reception rooms, unlit but for what little light dribbles in from the hallways, we roam. In each one, a window, I'd say twenty feet high and ten feet wide, is completely covered with several finely applied layers of aluminum foil.

"What's with that?" I gesture with my head to Igor as he's turning round to make sure I'm not falling over anything in the dark. He utters the only four words I hear him say in the two times I see him that evening: "He don't like light."

The second time I see him, his body and being are paralyzed with fear.

But for now I'm delivered to an oddly well-lit small kitchen in the middle of which is a small, square breakfast bar around which people could sit if there were stools. Poor Igor makes himself scarce.

Enough minutes go by with no one coming that I feel safe to quickly peek in the cupboard under the sink to see what cleaning products Prince uses. After all, what woman wouldn't want her kitchen gleaming like a palace?

Actually, it is a bit of a mess in there, so I set about sorting it for him. Soon there's a *swoosh* sound and a sweet smell from somewhere behind me. I turn round. Prince is in the doorway. Ol' Fluffy Cuffs. Done up like the dog's dinner.

Seems like he's wearing literally all the makeup that was ever in history applied to the face of Boy George. Looks like I did when I went with Jerome Kearns to a school prom.

"You must be Shine-aid," he says.

"You must be Prance," I reply.

The breakfast bar is between us. He doesn't cross it. The refrigerator is to his right and to my left. "You want a drink?" He smiles.

"Yeah, anything nonalcoholic, please." It being the case I don't like alcohol because it makes me puke, and puking isn't a good look for Cinderella. It also being the case my granny taught me to always say please and thanks.

He turns his back to reach up in the cupboard for a glass. Then, quick as a flash, he spins round, slams the glass down so hard in front of me that I don't know how his hand doesn't go through it, and says, "Get it yourself."

I've seen this before. I grew up with it. I know it like the back of my hand. I start mentally checking for exits without taking my eyes off him.

I realize I don't know where I am. I never asked for an address. I don't know how to find the front door. It's dark. I don't know how to find a cab. I'm away off up in some hills very far from the highway is all I know. And it doesn't look like he's got me here for cake.

He commences stalking up and down his side of the breakfast bar, arms crossed, one hand rubbing his chin between his thumb and forefinger as if he has a beard, looking me up and down like (a) I'm a piece of dog shit on the end of his shoe, and (b) he's figuring out where upon my little body to punch me for the fullest effect.

I don't like this. And I don't appreciate it. And I don't appreciate the assumption I'm easy prey. I'm Irish. We're different. We don't give a shit who you are. We've been colonized by the very worst of the spiritual worst and we survived intact.

Accordingly, when he shouts at me, "I don't like the language you're using in your print interviews," I say, "You mean English? Oh. I'm sorry about that, the Irish was beaten out of us."

"No," he says. "I don't like you swearing."

"I don't work for you," I tell him. "If you don't like it, you can fuck yourself."

This reeeeeeeeeaaaalllly pisses him off. But he contains it in a silent seethe.

He leaves the kitchen and I hear him call several times for someone named Duane. His voice is farther away each time he shouts so I know I have a moment to look for a back door. No luck. And soon I hear the footsteps of himself and also Igor returning.

Before they can get to the door, I hear him summon me. I'm to follow him up a few steps into a tiny dining area. This I do, noticing as I pass Igor that he's keeping his eyes to the floor, very frightened, his body frozen in subservience.

I sit at the table. I'm facing toward the courtyard. Himself is to my left. He shouts a violent order down the few steps to Igor. He wants soup. He asks if I want any. I really don't wanna be part of treating Igor badly, so I say I'm not hungry.

It's very, very low light where we are sitting. We aren't saying anything. He's brooding. He shouts again, and after a while poor Igor shuffles up the steps, carrying a silver tray that is draped with cream linen and upon which stutter two bowls of soup and two spoons. He is carrying himself as if he's a battered child about to get beaten again. His hands are shaking and he is cowed as if before a demon. It's the same abject fear my mother induced so often in my little brother. Igor looks like he's ready to piss his pants. He also seems woozy, as if drugged.

He stands at the table in front of his master. He doesn't lower the tray. Maybe twenty seconds go by. His head is down. Looks like Oliver Twist asking for more.

"You may put it down now," says himself. This Igor does. Then stands back with his hands held as if there is a cap in them. For some reason, I know what's about to happen.

"Serve Ms. O'Connor some soup," himself barks at Igor.

"I don't want any soup, thanks," I answer politely, patting my belly and looking at Igor as if to say, *I'm sure it's delicious but I'm stuffed* (just as my granny taught me). Igor's head doesn't move but his eyes flash to me and then himself and back to the floor.

Rather like Mrs. Doyle in the BBC sitcom *Father Ted,* himself then begins repeatedly insisting to Igor that he serve me soup. Only, unlike Mrs. Doyle, he spoke in such a demeaning and humiliating manner that poor Igor shook more and begged me with his eyes to let him serve me the stupid soup. But every time he moved toward me with the bowl, I held my hands up and said, "No, thanks."

Igor knew what was going on. I wasn't going to be part of humiliating him. I wouldn't have eaten the soup if my life depended on it. He finally placed the bowl back on the tray and stood holding the lot, not knowing what to do, looking like he was gonna cry.

Silence for some moments, Igor waiting for his lashing. It finally comes. Himself turns his vicious little face to mine and says, in a tone normal people would use when discussing feces, "This, by the way, is my brother Duane."

I'm stunned. And I'm disgusted that he could treat his brother so badly. I express this as poor Duane fades out of the room. Things get heated.

At some point himself decides we need to calm down, and he goes upstairs, I'm thinking presumably to powder his nose and make sure Dorian Gray's portrait is still okay in the attic.

He comes down with two pillows and says, "Why don't we have a pillow fight?" All smiles and nice. I think, *Okay, it wouldn't be every day that you'd get to have a pillow fight with Prince, what the hell, let's try to make it a fun evening after the shitty start.*

Only on the first thump I get, I realize he's got something in the pillow, stuffed down the end, designed to hurt. He ain't playing at all.

I get really annoyed. And also really frightened. A few more thumps get exchanged and he goes upstairs again. By this time, we've somehow arrived beside the front door. I open it and run out. The driver is there in the parked limousine, heavily asleep. I don't want to wake him. But there's a huge gate, locked. I begin quietly calling for Duane. I run to the right, where the outbuildings are, thinking maybe he lives there.

Next thing there's a *swoosh* and a sweet smell, and there's himself behind me. He orders me back in the house. And I obey. This is all too familiar for me to accept without protest, needless to say. I wish to leave and am told I may not.

After a while, he informs me that I may open the front door and tell his driver to take me home. I open the door so that there is some decent light and say I do not wish to wake the driver, that I would prefer to call a cab. Another temper tantrum ensues. How dare I not do as he is telling me? He stomps upstairs again.

Right inside the front door there is a small chair. When he comes back down, he throws himself on it and sits staring at the floor, saying nothing for maybe two minutes. I stand very close in front of him, trying to reason with him about how I really don't feel very safe right now and would like to be in control of the manner in which I get home.

He lifts his face up to mine, as close as six inches, and stares into my eyes for like ten seconds. From the light through the open door, I see his eyes clearly. His irises dissolve in front of me, so that his eyes go pure white. They don't go up. They don't go down. They don't go left. They don't go right. They dissolve. I see it clear as day. I get a cold fear in my stomach. I run out the door again and shake the driver awake through his open window while yelling for Duane.

I hear Duane's shuffle coming from the vicinity of the outbuildings but before he can get to me and before the driver has both eyes open, himself has me by the elbow.

He orders Duane to back off and tells the driver to go to bed. They both do as they're told.

Himself literally drags me toward the front door and orders me to stand on the step while he finds his car keys. No way in hell am I getting in a locked vehicle with this motherfucker, so I make a run for it round the left of the building and get about five hundred feet in the darkness.

I think I've gone beyond the boundaries of the property. There are some palm trees. I hide myself behind one and turn my head to see where he is. Seeing nothing, I take off my outer top, which is light-colored. Underneath I'm wearing black. He won't see me. He'll be looking for what I was wearing.

I hear him stomp about at the front of the house. Shouting but still not knowing how to pronounce my name. All he could do was say, "Where the fuck you gone?" I hear the ground crunch a little in my direction. But he decides to go back and get in his car.

He drives down the winding hill. I can see him clearly because of the car's lights. They also illuminate my pathway enough that I make a move from tree to tree each time he disappears down a bend, and after about half an hour I see the lights of a highway.

By the time I make it all the way down, the sun is making its way up. I'm relieved. Everything is silver-lit. I troop along, head hanging, trying to thumb a lift back to Los Feliz. Horribly familiar, the walk and the whole experience. I might as well have been in Glenageary. All the time, I'm looking to make sure it ain't him that stops to give me a lift.

Next thing it fuckin' *is* him. He drives alongside me, rolls down the passenger window, and orders me to get in, his left hand limp across his pimp rest. I tell him he can suck my dick. Or some such.

He screeches the car to a halt in the slow lane and gets out. Starts chasing me round the car, telling me he's gonna kick the shit out of me (as if I hadn't spotted clue one at ten p.m.).

I chase him back, and we run around the car for a few moments, him furious not to be able to catch me, me spitting at him like a cat that just had babies.

I've been walking long enough that there are now houses on each side of the highway with driveways of only about six feet in length. I recall my father telling me once that if ever I found myself in such a situation with a man, I should (after declaring my father is a policeman) ring someone's doorbell if possible and get help. And this I decide to do.

First I run around after the stupid bastard enough to observe his

159

pattern. I know when I'll get my break because he has to look to his right for a second before he runs into the road. Soon as he does that, I bolt up a drive and ring the first doorbell I come to and just keep ringing it.

He jumps back in his car (my father was right). He sits and watches me for a minute as if, in the event of no answer, he is contemplating another few laps. But he decides not to take the risk. He doesn't like light. Someone might have seen him. He turns the car around and speeds off. Doesn't bother looking left at me as he passes.

I walk ages more because no one answers at the house. I know he is gone.

When I get to the first phone booth, I call my friend Ciara, who is living with me. She comes to pick me up. I'm about forty minutes away from home.

After I tell Steve Fargnoli, he goes berserk. He wants to go round and shoot Fluffy Cuffs. As does another of his Italian-American friends. They say I've been the victim of an attack that was actually meant to terrorize Steve.

Apparently there's some legal proceedings going on between him and Prince. I dunno anything more about it. I don't care either.

I never wanted to see that devil again.

But I think of Duane fondly, quite often.

Sinéad with her manager, Steve Fargnoli
JOHN REYNOLDS

THAT'S WHY THERE'S
CHOCOLATE AND VANILLA

BESIDES BEING A GREAT music manager, Steve Fargnoli ran a few what I can only describe as legal whorehouses. The law was in England, you could have one working woman and one secretary. There'd be a "normal sex" room and a "beat me up" room. Steve was a pimp. He didn't avail himself of the women's services. But they availed themselves of him. By which I mean, he funded these people, largely because he was a sucker for what he called "the Underbelly" and for beautiful women with sob stories. The whore business isn't at all unlike the music business, by the way. In fact, they are the very same. He called me one Thursday to cancel a meeting we'd arranged for the following day. "I can't make it," he says. "We're putting in a dungeon tomorrow night, the cross is arriving." That's just what he did with his 20 percent. It was sweet, and amusing.

That's what I don't call one of the ladies who was in his office one Friday night, close to Christmas. An unpleasant blond woman. A dominatrix, violent of spirit, who almost murderously despised men. Including Steve, and indeed she had Steve's office burgled a few times by her other handlers despite his having taken care of her. He really was a sucker. Innocent-hearted. Blinded by the boobs and the baby talk. There really are guys like that. (Or used to be.)

Anyway, this lady pulls out a letter from one of her regular clients when I start asking her about what she does and how it all works. She tells me the guys who want the weird stuff don't want it for sexual purposes, it has nothing to do with sex; they just wanna get treated like shit. She adores treating them like shit. Not for her sexual purposes either. Just 'cause she's a total bitch.

The letter says the guy is gonna miss her over Christmas and he's gonna be practicing his "barking techniques" while she's away. Call me old-fashioned, but I had to ask her what on earth he was on about. She says every evening at seven he calls her from his office and she has him bark like a dog on the phone (I'm thinking, *What about the cleaners?*). She says he comes round and the deal is she treats him like a dog. She loves to kick him about. She says she makes him lap up bowls of her pee just to take it further than he intended and she gets off on humiliating him. Making him crawl around on his hands and knees like a dog. She's horrible. Really horrible. Then she can put on this act of "the lovely other woman" when the "normal sex" dudes turn up. She'd knife her own granny is the truth. These poor guys have no idea who or what they're in the presence of.

Steve's been my manager for about twelve years. I met him in the Camden Palace after a Prince show to which I had for some reason received an invitation. It was shortly after my first album came out and quite some time before the song "Nothing Compares 2 U" ever entered my ether.

He was born in Newport, Rhode Island. His father was a grocer. For some reason the father gave everything he owned to Sly Stone so he could go on tour. And Sly didn't go on tour, so Steve's father went broke. Steve as a teenager went to Los Angeles, tracked Sly down, and battered his door in. Forced him out on the road so Steve's father was paid back the money. That's how Steve got into the music business. Actually, before that, he worked at the Newport Jazz Festival; his job was to knock on Ella Fitzgerald's door and say, "Five minutes, Miss Fitzgerald." He told me he was a singer in a band once but he gave up when he saw Robert Plant singing. Said there was no point continuing.

After Prince's Camden Palace show, the next time I saw Steve was at a picnic on Hampstead Heath with some friends of his. For no reason other than social. It was sunny and nice. He was fun, the kind of person who would make you not want to wander home. When things broke down between myself and Fachtna, I asked Steve to take over, and he did so very passionately.

He looks like a teddy bear. He has white hair and chubby cheeks and is plump in an Italian-guy-who-loves-food way. He wears thick glasses and he literally can't see a thing without them. His tiny little mother's name is Rose and sometimes she'd invite us and his stable of girls all over to the house in Malibu and she'd cook just zillions of dishes. He looks after her like she is gold dust. And she is. He adores her.

His father has been dead a long time. Steve is everyone's father. Except his actual daughter's.

That's an issue between us sometimes, that he didn't have enough to do with his child.

Anyway, Steve loves lap-dancing clubs and ladies generally. So we all tagged along with him and his friends (one of whom I'm insanely in love with) to the clubs in Atlanta one night and marveled at the boob jobs. I can tell you there absolutely *is* sex in the champagne room.

Janet Street-Porter, the journalist and broadcaster, is in love with Steve. But they're best friends. All of us are a bit in love with him. But he doesn't care for sex et cetera from anyone or anywhere. He's in love with some extraordinarily high-maintenance German bird who works for MTV. But she's always breaking his heart. She does the "reach and withdraw" technique better than any man. Up until a while ago she was threatening to marry the Pakistani powerhouse Imran Khan. She was going around wearing a hijab. But he's just gone off and married Jemima Goldsmith. So it's all high drama and Steve says now she wants looking after. He drinks green alcohol when we're out and she's around so he's blasted. He's like a little boy in a sweet shop.

Reason Steve's a target is he's stinking rich. Remember, he used to manage Prince. And he has other businesses, all honest and aboveboard.

He's a person who does good. All the high-maintenance ladies want a rich dude. Only problem is, if you get Steve, you get all the rest of us as well — and of course you have to get past Janet Street-Porter. That is no easy task. She'd be a good match in all honesty because she's stinking rich too and she loves him. She doesn't want him for the reasons all the high-class ladies want him. Steve and her make each other laugh. He does love her. But he loves all women. That's the deal with Steve. He ain't boyfriend or husband material.

I respect Steve to the hilt otherwise. He's an angel sent from heaven. And I really wish heaven didn't want him. He's had cancer, and the doctors had him running all over town having all manner of horrible and pointless surgeries. He's gone through two years of hell for nothing.

It is common for music-business people to feel truly at home only in hotels. Steve doesn't have a home. He loves five-star hotels and he has lived in those. Circling around, as it were. Trying them all.

In 2001, in the W Hotel in LA, he lies dying. Every day behind reception downstairs is a different beautiful young woman stretched out in a human-size fish tank (which is empty of water, thank God). Playfully pulling at the fluffy turquoise shag pile, she's wearing a bikini. All the better for seducing with uplifted eyes the gentlemen as they check in. The whole scenario is very Fargnoli, as we who adore him would say.

I really don't know what will become of any of us now.

The millisecond his best friend, Arnon, stepped into the lift after saying goodbye, there was a tiny earthquake. Lasted about seven seconds. I know it was his grief. Don't care what anyone says. The man's poor heart was broken. In the desert. And God was with him.

Protesting abuse: Sinéad ripping Pope John Paul II's
photo on Saturday Night Live, *1992*

WAR, PART ONE —
SATURDAY NIGHT LIVE, 1992

DOWN ON ST. MARK'S PLACE and Avenue A there's a tiny Irish bar run by a giant Irish man who has salt-and-pepper hair down to his shoulders, which stoop because he doesn't feel too good about himself. But he's an all right guy. He's kind. Yeah, he wears black all the time, and doom is in his features so that his face even looks like Ireland, but he loves his girlfriend so much that it lights up like England when he sees her.

Irish bars I hate, though. Nothin' but drunk people hanging on to your elbow, talking shite and crying. I don't like Irish music either, but I like me a smoke. So I sit outside on the pavement with coffee and hope the bastard cop with the stupid Prince Albert mustache who once kicked a spliff out of my hand doesn't show up. Supposedly, he's in the hooer's apartments above the stores, snorting coke when he's off duty. He'd be better off sticking to the spliff and not kicking the ladies.

One night about one a.m., I see that directly opposite the Irish bar a new juice bar has opened. A sign on the pavement says it stays open till the wee hours. I see there's lovely colored paintings on the walls and cheerful-looking oranges and apples piled up together at the cash register in a visual antithesis of Ireland.

People inside seem to be having quite the giggle. So I take up my equipment and wander over. Great balls of fire! I find several long-locked West Indians skinning up weed in fresh tobacco leaves and listening to Rasta music. Fuck the Irish bar; the juice bar becomes home.

From then on I go over to the Irish bar only for the purpose of quickly replenishing my coffee. The West Indians won't cross the twelve feet of road to sit in the Irish bar. They don't trust American people. And they don't trust coffee either.

They'd first thought I was a boy. Whole place all a-cackle when the truth was revealed. Happens I announce I'm in love with Robert Downey Jr. one evening. Horrified silent faces having uttered Bible quotes as to the wrongness of homosexuality become fountains of laughter after I, in equal horror at their thinking me male, open my coat and lift up my jumper so they can see my mangy Dunnes sports bra and pregnancy stretch marks.

I'm obviously ignorant in the Rastafari department. First thing the guy in charge of the "juice bar" had to point out to me was "not everyone who has locks is Rasta." More laughs. But he went on to prove it to me over time. His name is Terry. He's from St. Lucia. He's short, like me. Long locks. He's dark sallow, same color as peanut crunch. Tells me someone in his family way back shagged a "Chiney man." I tell him we have something in common, then, since I'm pale sallow because someone way back in my family shagged a Spaniard.

I'd fretfully fled to New York from London in the winter and I hadn't remembered to pack a coat. I was frozen. Terry drove all the way to his house and got me one of his. A huge black leather parka. Waaay too big for me. I was swamped in it. All the guys were laughing at me. But I love it more than any garment from Chanel. Because it's his.

He's become my teacher. I didn't ask him to be. He took it upon himself because I wouldn't shut up asking him questions about Rastafari. Sometimes the way he leans his head back and looks at me, puzzled, I know he's asking himself, *What is God trying to tell me via these questions?* But I don't know why he needs to ask. I feel worried. He gets terribly calm. Keeps folding the T-shirts and acting like the place really is just a juice bar.

He drives me round the outskirts of New York City in the early hours of the morning to eat ackee and saltfish with elderly Jamaicans who are grocers and fishmongers and butchers and such. "Backstage" in their stores or concrete warehouses, there's always an extremely well-worn sofa or two and a makeshift kitchen.

Not all the old men are Rastas, but the majority are. They range from, I'd say, forty to seventy. There's never fewer than three. They wait the night with one another. They don't fall asleep. God doesn't have to wake them and say, *Could you not keep Me company in My madness?*

Jamaicans don't do small talk. At first this is a bit uncomfortable because Irish people are always filling the gaps. I find myself in silence in fish-filled vans making deliveries, just like I did with my grandfather.

I thought they didn't like me was why they were silent. But it ain't anything other than they are watchers. They're watching out for God everywhere. They're like God's security detail. That's how they see themselves, and that is exactly how they are.

They're like Saint Michael leading God's angels to war against Satan. Like zillions of Saint Michaels all rolled into one huge pyre of prophecy. They're watching for the devil too. That's the enemy of God. The devil is their Lee Harvey Oswald. They only speak when it's about Scripture.

In the backs of their stores they call me "Sistah" or "Da-taah" as they hand me saucers of food. "Staat small," they say. It worries them I don't eat. I've just never been an eater. My blood is too anxious. The elders don't eat meat, but they eat fried fish and sweet potatoes and rice and peas. Rice and peas is actually rice and kidney beans cooked in coconut milk. Best thing a person could eat. I'm glad because I particularly hate peas unless I'm playing that game where each person puts a frozen pea in one nostril and holds the other nostril closed, and whoever manages to snot the pea out farthest is the winner.

The elders can't say *Ireland*. They call it *Irie-land*. They read from the Nevi'im, the biblical prophets, while I turn my face and scoff. Secretly loving the food but also feeling that painful humiliation from childhood that comes when I register hunger. It's too connected with my mother; I

171

can't accept it. Food turns to pebbles in my mouth, like Lot's wife looking back. I resist it, as if to prove I'm totally in God's hands.

But the elders are right. And they stress good food, not just food. They wooden-spoon more to me, laughing softly at the backs of their throats with pleasure when they see I've cleaned the saucer. They actually do treat me like a stray kitten. They say my whiskers are as white as theirs.

When I trust them, they decide to teach me. They do this without my even realizing it's being done. They don't sit me down and say this, that, or the other. They do it by the things they talk about with one another when I'm present.

They read from the book of Revelation and loudly discuss the fact it's about the end of religion. Hopping about, laughing for joy. Yelling, "Jah!" and "Rastafari!" and "Dread I!" with their arms up in the air, as if the prophecy has already been fulfilled.

The one thing they do direct at me is discussion of Ireland. "H-Englan' is natural h-enemee of h-Irie-lan'. Yuh not see dat?" I reply I'd have to be blind not to see it. They tell me, "An de pope is deh devil. So deh devil is deh reeel h-enemee."

They tell me, "Jah dwelling shall be on a earth among deh 'u-man race."

In Terry's juice bar there's a Rasta painting on the wall. There's an altar at the end of a long black-and-white-tiled cathedral floor. A skinny black king with the kindest face imaginable is seated on a massive golden throne replete with Amharic inscriptions. There are dark-skinned elders seated on both sides along the length of the floor. Misted. You can't tell who they are. Lions or ancient souls. A tiny woman in a white shift is standing at the foot of the throne, facing the emperor. Her right hand is outstretched. She's asking him to come into the city. His dais is so high above her, she reaches only to his knees. He relaxes in his chair and leans back on his elbow, tilting his head forward. Smiling kindly. Her skin is white and her head is shaved.

One early evening while I'm in New York to rehearse for *Saturday Night Live*, I'm gazing at the painting when suddenly Terry gestures for everyone to leave except me. Then he closes the shop door, pulls the shutters down quickly, and asks me to sit beside him right there on the floor. His face looks sorrowful as he takes my hands in his. He has something to tell me. He says he wants me to try to forgive him.

He tells me that he's soon gonna get killed. He says someone tried to kill him before, in a drive-by. He was in his car with some friends. Another car rolled up beside them and they shot at him seven times. He says they'll get him eventually.

I ask him why, and I can't bear the answer I get. He runs guns. And drugs. He's been using kids as mules. They have guns and drugs in their schoolbags, not books. He's moved in on someone's territory and it's only a matter of time.

I'm horrified. By what he's been doing and that he's going to be murdered. There is much pacing in the juice bar over the course of the week. That Friday night, he gives me a gold ring with a red oval stone on which is carved, most finely, a Roman soldier's head.

Fucking treacherous bastard. I could kill him myself. Not a Rasta on earth would touch seven thousand pounds of weed if it had a Roman soldier on it, never mind bejewel themselves with such a thing. I give it to Rufus, another Rasta, who, picking it up from my palm, repeatedly asks, "Why?" He thinks maybe I mean romance. I don't. I mean the soldier looks like him. Silly fucker takes this as a compliment! I realize in that millisecond what the rabbi meant back in London when he said, "Don't forget to leave the party before they all get drunk and start fighting." I climb the three heavy steps up from the shop onto St. Mark's Place, turn left onto Avenue A, and hail myself a cab.

The driver, softly clicking his tongue against his back teeth as if he were calling a puppy, pleads with me to consider having sex with him. I don't know where he imagines we're going to do it. Certainly not in the front seat. To say he's consumed a few too many patties would be an understatement. We're talking "American XXXL." I decline, informing him I've had a very unsexy evening. Sweetly, he sings me "Underneath the Mango Tree" to cheer me up as we push through the lights of Manhattan to my other world, wherein I pace the fluffy floors of my hotel suite until six a.m.

WAR, PART TWO —
GOTTA SERVE SOMEBODY

THE DAY MY MOTHER DIED, myself and my siblings went inside her house for the first time in several years. Our own secrets to seek. Not hers. There were still broken plastic swans in the bathroom. Resolute. Long-necked. Frozen. As if nothing had happened.

I took down from her bedroom wall the only photo she ever had up there, which was of Pope John Paul II. It was taken when he visited Ireland in 1979. "Young people of Ireland," he had said after making a show of kissing the ground at the Dublin airport like the flight had been overly frightening, "I love you." What a load of claptrap. Nobody loved us. Not even God. Sure, even our mothers and fathers couldn't stand us.

In 1978, Bob Geldof ripped up a photo of Olivia Newton-John and John Travolta on *Top of the Pops* because their shit record "Summer Nights" had been number one for seven weeks and finally Geldof's Boomtown Rats' single "Rat Trap" had taken over.

My intention had always been to destroy my mother's photo of the pope. It represented lies and liars and abuse. The type of people who kept these things were devils like my mother. I never knew when or where or how I would destroy it, but destroy it I would when the right moment came. And with that in mind, I carefully brought it everywhere I lived from that day forward. Because nobody ever gave a shit about the children of Ireland.

• • •

I've woken after going to bed at six a.m. It's one p.m. Only a few hours until camera rehearsal for *SNL*. I'm to perform two songs, the second of which is Bob Marley's "War," a cappella. The lyric is actually a speech given to the United Nations by the Ethiopian emperor Haile Selassie in New York in 1963 about racism being the cause of all wars. But I'm gonna change a few lines to be a declaration of war against child abuse. Because I'm pissed at Terry for what he told me last night. I'm pissed he's been using kids to run drugs.

And I'm pissed he's gonna be dead by Monday.

It also happens I've been pissed off for a few weeks because I've been reading *The Holy Blood and the Holy Grail* (a contrarian, blasphemous history of the early church) and also over a brief article, buried in the back of an Irish newspaper, hinting that children have been abused by priests but their stories are not believed by the police nor the bishops their parents report it to. So I've been thinking even more of destroying my mother's photo of JP2.

And I decide tonight is the night.

I bring the photo to the NBC studio and hide it in the dressing room. At the rehearsal, when I finish singing Bob Marley's "War," I hold up a photo of a Brazilian street kid who was killed by cops. I ask the cameraman to zoom in on the photo during the actual show. I don't tell him what I have in mind for later on. Everyone's happy. A dead child far away is no one's problem.

I know if I do this there'll be war. But I don't care. I know my Scripture. Nothing can touch me. I reject the world. Nobody can do a thing to me that hasn't been done already. I can sing in the streets like I used to. It's not like anyone will tear my throat out.

Showtime. I'm wearing a white lace dress that once belonged to Sade. I bought it at a rock 'n' roll auction in London when I was nineteen. Paid eight hundred pounds for it. It's beautiful. There's a coin-size lead weight in each side of the slit at the back, to keep it straight and make it hang ladylike.

Very clever. A dress for women to behave badly in. One day maybe I will have a daughter who gets married in it.

So the show goes on. First song, "Success Has Made a Failure of Our Home," is a dream. Plenty of people milling about backstage afterward —producers, managers, makeup artists, and fellow guests. I'm the flavor of the month. Everyone wants to talk to me. Tell me how I'm a good girl. But I know I'm an impostor.

Second song is set up beautifully. With one candle beside me and my Rasta prayer cloth tied to the microphone, I sing "War" a cappella. No one suspects a thing. But at the end, I don't hold up the child's picture. I hold up JP2's photo and then rip it into pieces. I yell, "Fight the real enemy!" (I'm talking to those who are gonna kill Terry.) And I blow out the candle.

Total stunned silence in the audience. And when I walk backstage, literally not a human being is in sight. All doors have closed. Everyone has vanished. Including my own manager, who locks himself in his room for three days and unplugs his phone.

Everyone wants a pop star, see? But I am a protest singer. I just had stuff to get off my chest. I had no desire for fame. In fact, that's why I chose the first song. "Success" was making a failure of my life. Because everyone was already calling me crazy for not acting like a pop star. For not worshipping fame. And I understand I've torn up the dreams of those around me. But those aren't my dreams. No one ever asked me what my dreams were; they just got mad at me for not being who they wanted me to be. My own dream is only to keep the contract I made with God before I ever made one with the music business. And that's a better fight than murder. I gotta get to the other side of life.

I am in my dressing room with my personal assistant, Ciara. We pack up my bags and leave the building. Outside 30 Rock, two young men are waiting for me and they throw a load of eggs at us both. But what they don't know is myself and Ciara are able to run a hundred meters in 11.3 seconds. So we run after them when they flee. We catch up with them in some alley. They are leaning, gasping for breath, against a black fence they didn't have the strength to climb. All we say, laughing at them, is "Hey, don't be throwing eggs at women." The two of them are so shocked at being chased and caught that they start laughing too, and it all ends very friendly. They straighten up and help us find a cab back to the hotel. The matter is being discussed on the news and we learn I am banned from NBC for life. This hurts me a lot less than rapes hurt those Irish children. And a lot less than Terry dying. Which happens on the following Monday anyway.

IT AIN'T NECESSARILY SO

A LOT OF PEOPLE say or think that tearing up the pope's photo derailed my career. That's not how I feel about it. I feel that having a number-one record derailed my career and my tearing the photo put me back on the right track. I had to make my living performing live again. And that's what I was born for. I wasn't born to be a pop star. You have to be a good girl for that. Not be too troubled.

I wasn't comfortable with what other people called success because it meant I had to be as others wanted me to be. After *SNL* I could just be me. Do what I love. Be imperfect. Be mad, even. Anything. I don't define success as having a good name or being wealthy. I define success by whether I keep the contract I made with the Holy Spirit before I made one with the music business. I never signed anything that said I would be a good girl.

I have supported my four children for thirty-five years. I supported us by performing live, and I became, if I may say so, a very fine live performer. So, far from the pope episode destroying my career, it set me on a path that fit me better. I'm not a pop star. I'm just a troubled soul who needs to scream into mikes now and then. I don't need to be number one. I don't need to be liked. I don't need to be welcome at the AMAs.

I just need to pay my yearly overheads, get shit off my chest, and not compromise or prostitute myself spiritually.

So no. It wasn't derailed. It was re-railed. And I feel I've been extremely successful as a single mother providing for her children.

THE CONDITION MY CONDITION IS IN —
1992, A FEW DAYS LATER

SO I CHECKED INTO the Chelsea Hotel this morning. It happens that none other than Dee Dee Ramone lives there, and he knocks on my door bearing not a pie or a cake but a few tabs of acid and asks would I like to partake.

I don't tell him I've never done it before, and I scarf down one tab while he scarfs down another. I notice he is very underweight. Doesn't seem he cares for food any more than I do, which is pretty much not at all. We go wandering into the streets of the city, heading we know not where and dancing to the music being played in various cabs we pass; we even stick our heads into one driver's open window because he's stuck in a traffic jam and blaring Ella Fitzgerald. He shows us the CD cover. She's all in pink and smiling. I hold the cover and read everything on it, both sides, like Aunt Frances taught me to.

Clearly, this is not Dee Dee's first rodeo when it comes to taking drugs, and his head is fucked. After an hour or two, he plonks himself on a step somewhere and starts acting like Sybil in the eponymous movie about multiple personalities: "The people, the people, the people." He thinks everyone is staring at him. They aren't. Or if they are, it's just because he looks like he's gonna pass out. He decides to go back to the

Chelsea Hotel and leave me on my own. I don't mind this arrangement. Means I'm free to go to St. Mark's and Avenue A. Which I duly do.

I meet my friend Rabbi at Terry's place. I don't know his real name. He's nicknamed Rabbi because he is always talking about God. He's a fiery Rasta-looking type, but very angry. Not a real Rasta. In fact, I wouldn't be surprised if he's bumped off a few people. He has a nasty streak in him. Sometimes I don't know why I hang out with him. I think it's only that he's interesting. He and I head to the park. It's still day-time. I find myself smiling at strangers. Acid is like that. Turns you back into a child, so you're open to people the way you were when you were small. A blond lady is smiling back at me. Sitting with her husband or whatever he is. I realize I must leave Rabbi and go back to the Irish bar when he starts feeling my hands in a manner that suggests he fancies a lap or two in the leaba (Irish for "bed"). I'm uninterested. I don't feel that way about him. Who wants to go to bed with someone so grumpy?

After that night, I don't do acid again until I'm thirty-three. In a rocka-billy club on London's Oxford Street with my friend BP Fallon, an Irish radio host. He loves rockabilly music. I can't bloody stand it. So I'm begging him can we please leave the club. He insists we have to stay. I'm stone-cold sober after an hour so I figure the acid is crap. As crap as the music. And I steal Beep's (his nickname is Beep) whole bag of acid, lock myself in the toilet, and scarf up the lot while he's banging on the door threatening to kill me when I exit. I'm laughing my head off as I eat every tab in the bag. Still, I'm sober as a judge after another hour. Nothing is happening. This is not acid, it's just some little cardboard squares and Beep has clearly been ripped off. Still, he won't leave the club and we end up staying there for a total of three hours. Finally, about midnight, he says we can go.

Well, as soon as my right foot hits Oxford Street—*whoooooosh!* I'm flying. The music hadn't let me trip because I hated it. I didn't know until this night how deep my relationship to music is. Cry-laughing (my favorite feeling in the world) and fascinated by the stars. We go to my house and light the fire. A fire looks like it's made of maggots when you're on acid. It's the weirdest thing. Makes me wonder if everything is secretly made of maggots. I get obsessed with letting the garden into the house and fling open all the windows in case it decides to accept my invitation. Never happens, of course. We just sit all night talking. At one point a bunch of flowers on my piano vanishes before my eyes and all I see is the word *monster*. But as soon as I realize that's just some bullshit in my mind, the flowers reappear and start dancing. So I learned to control my mind on acid far better than I could without it.

I did ecstasy a few times. Hated it. Crying the next day for anyone's mother. Curled up in a fetal position.

Same with coke. Twice I did it. Hated it. Next day crying like a cartoon, the tears not falling down my face but flying straight, horizontally. Nothing nice about it. Depressed and twenty dollars poorer. Not worth it at all. Took my manners.

Heroin I smoked once. It was disgusting. Never did it again.

Next drug I did was speed. In the nuthouse, believe it or not, in Dublin (I get to call it a nuthouse because I'm a nut. No one else gets to call it that). In the locked ward where they put you if you're suicidal, there's more class A drugs than in Shane MacGowan's dressing room. They never check the bags visitors bring. It's not like in America, where even your granny would be frisked up against a wall and chucked out if she brought you so much as a bottle of perfume. So, yeah, I'm on speed in there for one week, probably one of the happiest weeks of my life. Same thing two years later. One week on speed in the locked ward of the nuthouse. It made me want to write. I wish I had some now, in fact. But I vowed never to take it again because I loved it so much.

Alcohol and me have never been friends. I'm allergic. I just vomit. I must be the only Irish person in the world who doesn't drink. Last time I got drunk I was about twenty-three, again in New York. On St. Patrick's Day, in the Fitzpatrick Hotel, where plyboard had been nailed to the floor in the bar to protect the carpet from puking, rowdy Paddies who had come from Ireland just to get drunker than skunks.

Irish coffee it was, with horrible crème de menthe shamrocks squirted on top. Well, I hugged the toilet all night while the room spun and I puked. And I was so tired but couldn't sleep because of all the coffee. I was still puking the next day. And I have not touched a drop of alcohol since.

I found all these drugs very easy to abandon, for which I am very lucky.

It's weed I wasn't sober on. On weed, I was always working. And I loved it. Because I could stay in my own world when the world outside me didn't make sense. Most musicians love weed because it turns up the music inside you and helps you cope with all the hanging around doing nothing, it being the case that weed makes doing nothing interesting. Hotels, dressing rooms, buses, airports, working two and a half hours of the day, the rest spent relentlessly waiting.

Yes, weed I've liked too much.

HOMELESS MAN AT EASTER

THE MOST INCREDIBLE human being I ever met was a homeless man whose name I didn't even get. Forgive me if that rhymes. It was not long before my *SNL* appearance, on Good Friday in a diner full of white people in New York.

In the door came this African-American man wearing a long, long army-type trench coat and, around his neck, a jack-to-jack lead, which is a lead that connects a guitar to an amp.

I was sitting at the bar part of the diner, and all the other white eaters were sitting in their booths, and this man wasn't fit for their company. So the boss of the diner turned him round and walked him out, and I was quite shocked because this is not something that would happen in my own country.

Next minute—about five minutes later, rather—he returned. And he did what I thought was the most incredible thing for a human being to do. He came back into the restaurant, stood about six feet inside, opened up his arms, and said, "Can I get a hug? Can I just get a hug?"

Genius, I thought. And I ran up to him and leaped on him like a monkey. And I was the only person who did. I jumped into his arms and hung on to him as if I were a baby, wrapping my legs around his waist. I hung on to him for a very long time.

We then went outside and had some conversation. I can't remember what we talked about, but afterward, he gave me the jack-to-jack lead that he had around his neck.

It has been lost somewhere in some house move at some point. But it was a treasured possession of mine for a long, long time afterward. I had it hung on my bedroom wall. And I often think about him. What a genius. "Can I get a hug?"

Bob Dylan performing at his anniversary concert
COURTESY OF COLUMBIA RECORDS

WAR, PART THREE —
OCTOBER 1992

I'M SO EXCITED. I get to sing at the Madison Square Garden concert celebrating Bob Dylan's recording career. I think I've been asked because I've said in every interview I've ever done that he's been a huge influence on me, spiritually speaking.

His song "Gotta Serve Somebody" is my road map for what kind of artist I want to be—not just an entertainer but an activist.

Indeed, I wouldn't have ripped up the pope's picture two weeks ago if not for that song and what it says musicians must do.

At the rehearsal the day before, Willie Nelson sidles up to me and asks if I will record Peter Gabriel's "Don't Give Up" with him the day after the show. I'm thrilled. If my mother weren't already dead, she would die! She loved Willie Nelson so bad.

The song I'm to perform at Madison Square is "I Believe in You" from Bob's album *Slow Train Coming*. When the album was released, I had not seen my father for some time because my mother was preventing it and the courts in Ireland were shitty to fathers. So I was without elder male guidance. The album became my father figure.

When I first try to sing "I Believe in You," I cry my eyes out, it means that much to me. I always know I'm gonna sing a song well if at first it makes me blubber. Same happened with "Streets of London." Had to run out of the room three times. Same with "Don't Cry for Me Argentina" and "Scarlet Ribbons." Some songs you just even think about them, you cry. Like "America the Beautiful."

Anyway, because I get so emotional, Booker T. and his band, who were the house band for the night, and myself come up with what is a very soft and whispered version, vocally speaking. There won't be a dry eye in the house.

And all I want is for Bob to be proud of it.

Morning of the show, I buy an outfit from Bergdorf Goodman. Only because I like the color—turquoise. Because turquoise represents communication in the world of mediumship.

I don't try the outfit on at the store. And when I get back to the hotel, I don't try it on for hours. When I finally don it and look in the mirror, I see it's really for someone in the television show *Dynasty*. You gotta have a bouffant to get away with these shoulder pads, and I'm bald as an egg. And the matching skirt shows my hideous ballet legs. I look ridiculous. And very underweight. Because I rarely eat. But it's five o'clock now and it's too late to find something else. So I tell myself the mediumship of the color is all that matters. And I know it's true.

But when I walk onstage that night and half the audience starts booing, for a second I actually think it's the outfit, because in my excitement at being part of the show, I've forgotten all about the pope-photo incident on *SNL*.

Then the other half of the audience begins cheering to fight off the booers. And there ensues a noise the likes of which I have never heard and can't describe other than to say it's like a thunderclap that never ends. The loudest noise I've ever heard. Like a sonic riot, as if the sky is ripping apart. It makes me feel really nauseous and almost bursts my eardrums. And for a minute or two I'm not sure the audience members aren't going to actually riot. They're clashing so badly already with their voices. How do I know what else might happen?

I pace awhile onstage. I realize that if I start the song, I'm fucked, because the vocal is so whispered, both sides in the audience's battle are going to drown me out. And I can't afford to not be heard; the booers will take it as a victory.

I look at Booker T.'s beautiful face. He's mouthing the words *Sing the song*, but I don't.

Now I'm asking God what I should do. I keep pacing, which becomes uncomfortable for everyone backstage because the show's got to go on as planned, so someone dispatches Kris Kristofferson (this he tells me later) to "get her off the stage." As he's making his way there, I get my answer from God: I'm to do what Jesus would do. So I literally scream the biggest rage I can muster, the Bob Marley song "War" to which I tore up the pope's picture. And then I almost get sick.

I see Kristofferson walking up to me. I'm thinking, *I don't need a man to rescue me, thanks*. It's so embarrassing. "Don't let the bastards get you down," he says into my mike. And we go offstage and I almost barf on him as he gives me a hug.

Afterward, I feel like Bob Dylan is the one who should have come out and told his audience to let me sing. And I'm pissed that he didn't. So I glare at him in the wings as if he's my big brother who's just told my parents I skipped school. He stares back at me, baffled. He's looking all handsome in his white shirt and pants. It's the weirdest thirty seconds of my life.

The day after Madison Square Garden I go to visit Dylan's manager in his office. I tell him about what's been happening in the church in Ireland, that kids have been raped and the church is covering it up. I ask if he and Dylan will help expose it. He thinks I'm crazy. Offers no help. Neither he nor Dylan are gonna speak up for me. I'm on my own. (I wonder if they still think I'm crazy now.)

My father, who was in the audience that night, advises me afterward that it might be time for me to reconsider college because I just destroyed my career. He's right. But I don't care. Some things are worth losing your career for. And I don't want a pop-star career anymore anyway because nobody knows me and I'm so lonely.

SUSIE DAVIS

Sinéad disguised as a protester against herself

SUSIE DAVIS

MY STAR-SPANGLED BANNER

THE BLOWBACK AFTER *SNL* was stronger than it had been a couple years earlier with another controversy.

It's 1990, and over the past few days, I've seen some news footage in my hotel rooms that's made me cry-laugh. I'm on tour in America, and in some towns and cities, people have been steamrollering piles of my albums at intersections.

"Bring Us Your Sinéad O'Connor Album and We'll Crush It for You" has been the arrangement. Forward, reverse, forward, reverse, over the little hills of CDs. Intensely angry old people (with very pointy noses) operating the steamrollers. I don't think I've ever seen anything so funny. Nor has the Irish artist in me ever been more proud, especially today when, wearing a pair of sunglasses and a wig outside the venue at New York's Saratoga Performing Arts Center, between sound check and showtime, I had the great joy of joining with my best friend, Ciara, in a protest against myself. In fake American accents, we chatted with the five or so Vietnam veterans who were the only other people who'd turned up at a protest promoted by a local disc jockey.

They were "large," shall we say, all male, and three of them were wearing black-framed, enormous round spectacles with lenses so thick, their eyes looked humongous. They had painstakingly made and were proudly carrying placards that left no one in any doubt that they felt I should leave America immediately and that ALL SINÉAD O'CONNOR LOVES ABOUT AMERICA IS THE DOLLAR.

Needless (I hope) to point out, they were mistaken. Only an eejit wouldn't love America. Plus only an eejit would leave America for any reason other than deportation. Whatever else I might be fairly or otherwise accused of, I am a gazillion percent secure in my status as a non-eejit. More now than ever, because if I were an eejit, no one would need to be steamrollering my records.

This is a very good thing.

Ciara and myself agreed passionately with the protesters that "Shine-Aid O'Caaanerrr" and her ilk should "Git baayack t' Eye-errr-layand." And that "she is jest a evul woman tryin' t' cor-rupt our keeyuds with herr disreeeespeck." And that "no way can she be Christeeyan!" We even had our pictures gloriously taken with them for their scrapbooks. They were so proud that two such nice young ladies would support them, poor creatures.

After twenty minutes or so, we ladies clambered onto a wooden fence and just sat watchin' them continue to do their thang, walking up and down with the placards. A news crew had turned up because elements of the media had been trying to drum up a huge protest in the previous days. But as it happened, that failed, and the guys were the only protesters for them to film.

Next thing we know, a local female TV reporter (brunette, wearing six years' worth of makeup) wanders over to us with her cameraman and her sound guy, who is carrying a ridiculously phallic fuzzy microphone above her head. "Ex-kee-use me, miss, arr ewe frum aroun' hee-urr?" she asks.

I decide to say "Uhhh" for a very long time. Then I venture, "Ahhm frum Sarah-toga." Ciara and me both try not to snot laughing or look at each other. "Watt's ewe-er nayme?" the reporter asks. "Uhh. Ah preferrr neverrr t' give mah nayme t' strrangerrrs," I say. We barely manage not to fall off the fence.

Luckily, they went away quickly. We were too bizarre. But they ran it later on the news, with the caption *Is that her?* Running and rerunning the footage of my "interview." Aha-ha-ha-ha-ha!

This silliness all transpired because a couple months back, before I was to go onstage in some venue in New Jersey, two Caucasians (as they say in America), one male and one female, came to my dressing room. They asked me how would I feel about "The Star-Spangled Banner," the American national anthem, being played through the speakers before I perform.

Now, mea culpa, but because where I come from we speak English, I gleaned from the phrasing of their question and from the fact they *put* it as a question at all that what they were saying was if I didn't feel cool about it, that would be cool. No American anthem? No problem.

Between you and me? Anthems have petrifyingly contagious associations with squareness unless they're being played by Jimi Hendrix. Also, for the most part, people come to shows so they can forget about the outside world, not be reminded of it. But I had about ten minutes till stage time and I needed to get my wires down the back of my shirt and take the usual last few panic pees, so I just said that, given the choice, I'd prefer it wasn't played. I didn't give them any explanation. They sweetly smiled and said that was "just fine" and that I should "have a great show."

But the whole thing was an extraordinary setup. While I was onstage, the two sleeveens called a local television news show and created a nationwide fuss by falsely reporting that I had sought them out and demanded the anthem not be played before the show. They also claimed that I told them I would not go on if it was played. Which is entirely untrue. One's tour insurance would never cover one for such a decision (I told you I'm no eejit).

Media frenzy ensues. Sinéad, the Hater of America. Right at the height of my tour.

MC Hammer, cashing in on the whole thing, publicly sends me a check for a first-class ticket back to Ireland. The check, like him, reeks of coconut. Even I can see it's also cavalier businessmanning on his part.

Years from now, the thing is gonna be worth a lot more than the fifteen hundred or so dollars he's written it for.

Actually, come to think of it, there is one reason to leave America: MC Hammer's videos. Christ Almighty.

Frank Sinatra weighs in and opines I should have my ass kicked, which is worrying because I'm staying in the same hotel as him. We might happen across each other in the lift, and I'm thinking my father back in Dublin isn't gonna be too pleased if I tell him I had to, in self-defense, beat the crap out of Ol' Blue Eyes.

I start checking my bed for horse heads.

I'm feeling flattered that the Establishment considers me enough of a threat that it needs to try and discredit me along with all the other bands and artists who have been under attack in this censorship of music that is America since *Straight Outta Compton*. Clearly, we're all onto something. Clearly, we've all been onto it all along. I know what it is too. We're like the mirror in *Snow White*.

PART THREE

SOME MUSICAL NOTES

I'M CERTAIN PART of the reason I became a singer was that I couldn't become a priest, given that I had a vagina and a pair of breasts (however insignificant). I always had an interest in working with dying people, because I was always a person who believed very much in an afterlife and in the lack of need to fear death, which I discerned from having had the Gospels drilled into me. I figured that was Jesus's reason for coming to Earth. That seemed to sink in to such a degree that only now, as I'm writing about my songs, have I become aware that an awful lot of them are about death or talking to dying people or where the narrator is a dead person.

The very first song that I ever wrote, in fact, "Take My Hand," featured an angel singing to a dying old man: "Come with me. Everything's going to be rosy." It was an unusual subject for a fourteen-year-old to be writing about.

I've written a lot in this book about my upbringing and my youth and how it is I came to be an artist. But I have not yet written much about the individual songs or albums. I thought it might be useful to relate all the information that I can concerning those. I always say that if one could discuss music, one wouldn't need music, since music is for the things that cannot be discussed.

Please be aware that every album represents a diary and each song

199

is a chapter in that diary. And my collection of albums represents my healing journey. When I was younger, I wrote from a place of pain, because I needed to get things off my chest. Once I came to the *Theology* album, which is all Scripture, I worked from a place of healing. And the first album I wrote totally from that platform is *I'm Not Bossy, I'm the Boss*. And it is from that platform I continue to write. After all, there is no point setting out on a healing journey if you're not going to find yourself healed.

And it is also the case that if anyone wants to truly know me, the best way is through my songs. There is nothing I could write in this book or tell you that would help you get to know me. It is all in the songs.

I DO NOT WANT
WHAT I HAVEN'T GOT

"JACKIE" WAS THE SONG I remember writing after "Take My Hand"; I was about fifteen, and it ended up on *Lion and the Cobra*. I had seen a play on TV about a very old lady in Scotland who was coming toward her own death. She would spend her days looking through her curtained window, waiting to see her long-gone husband return from a fishing trip he'd taken forty years earlier and during which he'd drowned. They had been childless, and she never met anyone else.

This inspired me, somehow, to write "Jackie," about a character who is wandering the beach waiting for the return of someone dead. In my song, the narrator is a ghost.

People always assume my songs are autobiographical, but that's true only about 50 percent of the time. They often guess wrong, especially when they presume a song is about mental illness. Though this doesn't really apply to "Jackie." It's interesting that this song falls into a category of lyrics sung from the point of view of people who have passed on. I seem to have had, even then, an interest in the afterlife, a nonbelief in the finality of death, that concerned me musically as well as spiritually.

It is all, as I said, because I didn't get to be a priest. I should have been a missionary, in fact, but the next best thing was music.

As I mentioned, "Drink Before the War" (I have no idea where that title came from!) emerged from my anger at my headmaster in Waterford who hated me wanting to be a musician. I didn't give a shit, and the headmaster was a snob and a cowardly little fucker. The song meant a lot to me when I wrote it, but I never perform it anymore because I feel embarrassed—singing it is like reading your teenage diary out loud.

I do still perform "Never Get Old," also written when I was fifteen or so and also on my first album. It is about the handsomest boy in school, Ben Johnson. All the girls wanted to go out with him because he was not only the best-looking boy but also the most mysterious. He trained hawks and was really sweet and rarely said a thing. As I wrote earlier, I finally got to go out with him one day; he took me to watch him and his hawk and we had the most amazing afternoon. I think we eventually kissed once or twice. And then I got dumped, though it was done very nicely. I was probably a terrible kisser. But I was still quite upset. That's where "Never Get Old" came from.

"Mandinka" was inspired by the television series *Roots*, based on Alex Haley's novel about slavery. I was a young girl when I saw it, and it moved something so deeply in me, I had a visceral response. I came to emotionally identify with the civil rights movement and slavery, especially given the theocracy I lived in and the oppression in my own home.

Recording "Mandinka" was also a breakthrough for me musically. The recording was the first time I had the courage to play guitar properly; Chris Birkett, the producer, and Chris Hill from Ensign were very encouraging. The first time I played it for Chris Hill, I was sure he would think it was total shit. But as has often been my experience when I've gone to people with songs that I worried were absolute crap (such as "Reason with Me," about a character asking to be helped with life), people loved them. And I was proud that I'd managed to play guitar because, well, I'm not a great guitar player.

When I remember the tracks on *I Do Not Want What I Haven't Got*, I see again that the themes of death, dying, and communicating from the beyond are everywhere. In the first track, "Feel So Different," I'm actually talking to my mother. And "I Am Stretched on Your Grave," which is actually an old Irish poem, is very much about death. I used the famous James Brown drum track that was starting to appear on many rap tracks—the record company made me pay fifty thousand dollars for it, which I bet did not go to James Brown's drummer. I love singing it and always think about my mother when I do. Often, when I'm on tour, someone well known has just died, and I dedicate "Stretched on Your Grave" to that person.

A third death song is "Three Babies," about three miscarriages that I experienced. It is also about the four children I did have, though the song is perhaps a prophecy of not being the perfect mother. You have dreams of being a perfect mother to your kids, but maybe you don't always turn out to be one (though you get better as you get older).

"Black Boys on Mopeds" is based on a true story involving two young teenagers near where I lived in London. They had taken a cousin's moped without asking permission; the cops were called and gave chase; the boys got frightened, crashed, and died. This was at a time when there was a terrible scandal in London about Black men going missing in police stations. It was a time in London also when if a burglar was apprehended, he was reported as a "Black burglar" (or, alternatively, an "Irish burglar"). There was a lot of tension created between Londoners on the one hand and the Jamaicans and the Irish on the other.

The huge single from the album, my cover of Prince's "Nothing Compares 2 U," was a song I was always—and am always—singing to my mother. Every time I perform it, I feel it's the only time I get to spend with my mother and that I'm talking with her again. There's a belief that she's there, that she can hear me and I can connect to her. It's why I've cried on the line "All the flowers that you planted, Mama, in the backyard, all died when you went away." I love the song and never get fed up singing it.

The title track, "I Do Not Want What I Haven't Got," also came in a very dark and interesting way. I went to see a medium and my mother came through. My mother asked my sister to forgive her for what she had done to all of us. But my sister would not forgive her. And while I understood this, it made me very, very sad for my mother's soul. I was so young and didn't know any better.

That night I had a dream in which my mother came to me for the first time since she had died a year and a half earlier. In the dream, I told my mother I was sorry that Éimear couldn't forgive her. My mother said, "I do not want what I haven't got."

What my mother meant was that she didn't deserve my sister's forgiveness and that she knew she didn't deserve it so that I shouldn't feel sorry for her.

There's a lot going on around the issues of death and dying on my first and second albums. But I've also realized, hmm, there's an awful lot of songs about belief in the spirit world; it's not just "Oh, woe, woe, these are miserable songs about death." It's not like that. There are songs that are concerned with the idea that the Gospels are indeed such, and the Scriptures of old are true. And that there is no such thing as death, which is what all God's messengers have told us, no matter what religion they came from.

AM I NOT YOUR GIRL?

I WASN'T READY for the sort of success that came with *I Do Not Want What I Haven't Got*. It wasn't what I was looking for. I did not know how to handle it. It did my head in. I didn't know why anyone liked my songs. Singing them in front of every camera in the world, on every television show, I didn't know where I was; I wasn't with my kid. I didn't know who I was. I didn't feel comfortable in the whole pop-star role and with what the whole thing was doing to me.

I thought that, musically, I didn't want to be under the stress of a typical follow-up album. I really needed to come up with a red herring. I decided to buy myself some time so I'd be able to make the follow-up album that I really wanted to make, not the one that the record label demanded. A red-herring follow-up album would be so far fucking removed from pop-world expectations that nobody could compare it. So that's what I did with *Am I Not Your Girl?*

The album is filled with show tunes and jazz standards. The only thing that has any personal input from me is in Loretta Lynn's hit "Success Has Made a Failure of Our Home." Because that's really me talking about what success has done to my life. At the end, I made up some words that were very autobiographical. When the lyrics ran out, I suddenly started screaming, "Am I not your girl?" It was the only part of the album that I felt followed up *I Do Not Want What I Haven't Got*.

I also covered "Don't Cry for Me Argentina" because my mother always loved that song. And it meant the world to me to sing it. What meant the world to me too was a letter I got from Tim Rice, who wrote the lyrics, saying that my version was the best he had ever heard, hands down. And if my mother had not been already dead, she would have died of delight and pride.

"Scarlet Ribbons" is on the album. It's a song my father used to sing to me when I was a kid. That's why I'm crying singing it. It's so deep and meaningful to me. And my father singing that song to me really told me about the power of prayer and that miracles could happen. I was so blown away by the story of the song. I guess my father had a very sad singing voice too and he used to make me sad, the same way it made my daughter sad when I sang to her when she was little. When she heard my songs on the radio she'd say, "Too sad, turn it off, turn it off."

The esteemed vocal coach Frank Merriman

IRMANTAS BAUZA/THE BEL CANTO SCHOOL OF SINGING

UNIVERSAL MOTHER

I OFTEN THINK OF *Universal Mother* as the most special album I've ever made, for many, many reasons, one of which had to do with my father. He had been going for singing lessons for many years with a gentleman by the name of Frank Merriman who taught a style of singing called bel canto. It literally means "beautiful singing" and came from Italy in the early nineteenth century. It has nothing to do with scales or breathing or any of that kind of stuff. The whole concept is that the emotions take you to the notes. When I lived in London and made my first two albums, I sang in an American accent. I sang like all of the people I idolized. I never sang like just me. It had been very uncool in the 1980s to sing with an Irish accent, and in fact, Bob Geldof was the first person to do it.

I didn't begin to sing in an Irish accent until I went to see Frank Merriman as a student, which I did because I had dinner so often with him and my father when I happened to be in Dublin, and I was really impressed with what he had to say about singing. He described himself as a freer of voices, not a singing teacher, and he described singing as a spiritual study, which, in his presence, it really was. Studying with him led to the first time that I ever sang in my own voice, and I was able to say things that were really on my mind without having to code them as much as I had coded them in earlier albums. Frank freed more than just my voice; he freed my mind. In bel canto, you can't have one without the other.

Frank would make you sing opera arias, such as Puccini's "O Mio Babbino Caro," in a key that was way too high for you. Just when it got to the highest note and you knew you were going to make an absolute show of yourself, he would throw an apple or a tennis ball at you and you'd be so busy trying to either defend yourself from the thing or catch it that the note would come out of your body. It was his way of showing you that you were just in your own way; it was the Stanislavski method of singing. If you could just get yourself out of your own way, tell the story, feel the feelings, the notes were in you. Frank would say, "If a fire started in this room right now, you could yell *Fire* at the highest octave there is." But if you tried to sing that note when there was no fire, you wouldn't reach it.

So bel canto is all about seeing the pictures, telling the story, really believing it, and believing that the notes will take you to the emotions. It's nothing to do with learning how to breathe, nothing to do with the diaphragm, none of that. The only technical part is you must always vocalize in your own accent; as everyone's muscles are formed by the age of fourteen, and these muscles form the sound of your accent, it follows that you're going to end up in vocal trouble if you constrict your accent. That's why you see Bono, you see Adele, you see certain performers who have put on a fake accent having vocal trouble—they've constricted their vocal cords to act in a way that they're not built for.

In 1993, I moved back to Dublin to go to group vocal classes on Saturdays as well as study privately with Frank. In the group classes, there were maybe twenty people. Some of them just wanted to sing at parties. Some of them wanted to sing professionally. Some of them just wanted the joy of going to a singing class (like my father), and you would learn there that everyone's soul is individual and beautiful, but the ring in everyone's soul doesn't come out unless they're singing in their own authentic accent. And that's what is really beautiful.

It was from Frank's lessons that I developed a trick I sometimes still use onstage. I will tap my foot while performing and I'll be thinking about my foot. I won't be thinking about the notes that I have to sing, because if I think about the notes, I'm screwed. I think about anything but the notes that I have to reach.

It was during these lessons that I learned of the great sacrifices that the love of singing can lead a person to make. Frank is a man who, at a young age, went to Italy and lived on a park bench for a year because he couldn't afford a place to stay. He had only enough money to study there. Later, he came back to Dublin to be a teacher, thanks be to God.

Now, as I said, it was Frank who began to teach me to sing in my own voice and find my own spirit. Consequently, I started to talk about the things that I really wanted to talk about, and while *Am I Not Your Girl?* was officially my third album, it was really a red herring. On *Lion and the Cobra* and *I Do Not Want What I Haven't Got*, I sang about my upbringing, but I hadn't really said much. Now things would change.

Which brings me back to *Universal Mother*, from 1994. Most of the album was produced by Phil Coulter, who is a wonderful man whose nine children were each born nine months from the day that he got back from a tour. Phil is married to Geraldine Brannigan, a singer I admired very much growing up. Phil is a great piano player. He also wrote the song on the album called "Scorn Not His Simplicity."

One of the reasons I'm so proud of *Universal Mother* is that the Edge from U2 said he could listen to it only once, it was so personal. Nigel Grainge, as I wrote, said the same thing about the album that has "Nothing Compares 2 U" on it, *I Do Not Want What I Haven't Got*. He said it was like reading someone's diaries and that nobody would be interested. I think poor Edge felt differently. It was more that he felt all the pain in it. *Universal Mother* also received the best review an album of mine has ever gotten, written by the late Bill Graham, who worked for an Irish magazine called *Hot Press*. His review said it was the first time that anybody was singing about their family and that the topic of family was always taboo, but an artist like me, that's what I had been trying to get at all along. That was what I was getting at, but of course,

211

I was now singing in a different accent, acting like somebody else. It was all heavily coded. And it was obvious that this was a vulnerable girl and not necessarily the tough Bambi in bovver boots that everybody thought.

Now, I must admit I've never been so stoned in my life as I was in Amsterdam with Tim Simenon, who produced the tracks "Fire on Babylon," "Famine," and "Thank You for Hearing Me." Jesus, we smoked a lot of weed. I don't know how I managed to stay up on two feet, never mind sing.

"Fire on Babylon" is a song about my mother. I won't go into too much detail, but it had to do with something I found out she'd done to one of my brothers that just really made me angry. Truth to tell, it's very hard for me to get angry about my mother. It's the way I've survived. I've convinced myself she didn't know what she was doing. People will do that, but of course, I've misplaced that anger and it might be more mature for me to accept it. You can tell even from the video how furious with her I was as I present the poor mother figure with a birthday cake that blows up in her face.

I love "John, I Love You" very much. Love everything about it. People often think I wrote it about my brother John, but I didn't, though I do associate it with him sometimes. Here's the backstory: I had a piano teacher at Frank Merriman's school, John Stokes, whom I was madly in love with. Of course he wasn't interested in me at all because he was quite sensible and knew that I was completely out of my mind, that I was the last woman that any man should wish upon himself. Still, we were friends and I was really fond of him, loved him very, very much. I couldn't play piano and still can't; I have two elbows for hands when it comes to playing guitar, really, or piano. (Worse with piano, though.) Anyway, John Stokes is actually who the song is about.

"My Darling Child" is a song about my son Jake. Just really a lullaby and a love song. Of course, Jake has his own song on the record (for which he has a publishing deal), called "Am I a Human?" He was only about three, but he walked up to a microphone at his dad's house and suddenly out of him comes this incredible philosophy.

"Red Football" relates to the fact that this album was the first time in my life that I'd become myself and started to really look at what I'd been in the first twenty-two years of my life; it was finally dawning on me.

"A Perfect Indian" is a song about Daniel Day-Lewis; people think we had an affair but we never did. We were getting very friendly until I blew the friendship by losing my temper with him one night in a crazy way that I do sometimes. One of the effects of my childhood, unfortunately, so the song is as much about my upbringing as it is about Daniel. At the time, he was making the movie *The Last of the Mohicans*, so that's why it's called "A Perfect Indian." It's not that I was in love with him. (I wasn't.) But I was very fond of him as a friend. We're still very fond of each other, though I've seen him once in the last maybe twenty-five years.

The song "All Babies" is about the one and only rebirthing session that I ever went to, which completely blew my mind. It was like an acid trip—although I hadn't yet been on an acid trip—and I had the most magical experience. This song also influenced the painting on the album, which is the only cover art that I've ever done. That makes me wonder—where is that original drawing? Could be it's lost somewhere in the depths of Chrysalis or EMI or it's been sold or something, but I would certainly like it back.

"Thank You for Hearing Me," the final song on *Universal Mother*, I wrote about breaking up with Peter Gabriel. I had had an on-and-off fling with him in which I was basically weekend pussy—that would be the kindest way to describe it. And once I got fed up with being weekend pussy, I wrote this sort of split-up song. But it became, over the years, my favorite song to perform live because it just could take you, like a mantra, to these stratospheres of almost hypnosis.

I believe that Tim Simenon gave me the backing track. The entire band, every line, the bass line, the drums, the audience, we would all be in a trance with its repetition. It's very hard for me to describe where the song came from. It's quite a churchical—for want of a better word—experience, performing it. And I'm very, very proud of it as a breakup song, considering the fact that one is entitled to smash plates when one realizes one is being treated as weekend pussy.

As for "Famine," yes, I do remember going on a TV show in London and trying to perform that song in the midst of political tensions between Ireland and England; I was told that I shouldn't perform the song because it was too political. My folks said to the producer, "But hold on. If it was Bob Dylan here, you wouldn't say he couldn't perform 'The Times They Are a-Changin'.'" Nobody could do anything but agree. Eventually we did get to perform it live on British TV at least once. "Famine," of course, is a song about Ireland and how everyone believes there was a nineteenth-century famine, but in fact, there was lots and lots of food in the country, it was just being shipped out of the country. It was just that you were shot dead if you were Irish and you went near anything but a potato.

The fact is that to call it a famine is a lie. It was a controversial song and if I had not written it, I would not have met my daughter's father, who wrote about it very well. John Waters is his name, and we met to do an interview about that song. If we had not, if that song had not happened, our daughter, Roisin, would never have been born.

GOSPEL OAK

GOSPEL OAK WAS NAMED for the London neighborhood where I was visiting a therapist six days a week. His name was Morton Schatzman, a very old Jewish psychiatrist whose dog used to sit at his feet licking its balls. It was so embarrassing while I was sitting there trying to explain what was wrong with me. What I liked about Dr. Schatzman was he said you come to therapy to find out there's nothing wrong with you. But there was certainly something wrong with me when his dog was licking its balls. I'm Irish, so I was kind of uncomfortable, to say the least.

But I was very, very fond of this man, maybe even madly in love with him in lots of ways, as one can often be with one's therapist. And he was the only person who was nice to me then. I was very lonely, which was why I was going there six days a week. Probably I was lonely because I was a difficult personality. I didn't realize that at the time; I was young. Also because of my job, I guess.

Anyway, "This Is to Mother You" is the only song apart from "All Babies" that wrote itself. Sometimes artists will say they feel like they're channeling something. I don't feel that's what it is. What you're channeling, if anything, is your subconscious, which can be talking to you. And you have to be very careful what you write, because all songwriters will tell you that songs always come true. I just heard it inside myself and picked it out on the guitar and sang it.

A similar subconscious approach actually happened with all the tracks on *Gospel Oak*. "I Am Enough for Myself" was a meditation about things I was going through in therapy. It was a meditation and a set of affirmations about the way I wanted things to be.

"Petit Poulet" was my reaction to the genocide in Rwanda—I was horrified by what I saw on TV and this was my visceral reaction—and "4 My Love" is just that, a love song. "This Is a Rebel Song" was written in response to U2's "Sunday Bloody Sunday," which they would always introduce in performances with the words "This is not a rebel song." Maybe they were afraid it would be perceived as being about the war in the north of Ireland. And I wanted listeners to know that this was not only a love song, but a song about the war. But how do you tell the story of a war? It's good if you can make it look like you're talking about the relationship between a man and a woman.

"He Moved Through the Fair" (or "She Moved Through the Fair," as it's usually called) is on this record as well. It's a beautiful old Irish song, a ghost, and no one even knows who wrote it. I rerecorded it in a much higher key for the movie *Michael Collins*, and I like that version a lot as well.

Gospel Oak and *Universal Mother* are forever very linked for me because we toured the two albums together. We had the best fun on those tours.

Sinéad with Dave Stewart

FAITH AND COURAGE

FAITH AND COURAGE, which came out in 2000, was my fifth original album and my first original release in many years. Making the album was a great artistic and revitalizing act. It had been a difficult time. I was raising Jake and Roisin, became entangled in a hideous, very depressing custody battle over her, and attempted suicide on my thirty-third birthday.

I had great relationships with *Faith and Courage*'s many producers, especially Adrian Sherwood and Dave Stewart. In fact, myself and Adrian Sherwood were an item for a long time. I would work with Adrian on anything; I'd sing the phone book if he was recording it. He's the most incredible producer in the world as well as the greatest builder of spliffs; he would build me one and write sweet little love notes on the side.

On the record itself, "The Healing Room" is the same type of song as "Thank You for Hearing Me." It's a mantra and it takes people, hopefully, to another world. When I go onstage, I always pray that I can be a priest and that when I leave, people will feel like they've been at church. "The Healing Room" gives me that healing feeling.

"No Man's Woman" is just your standard pop song, and "Jealous" I simply love. It's one of my favorite tracks I've ever done; I did that one with Dave Stewart.

Also with Dave was "Daddy, I'm Fine." Dave had told me to go write a song about what it was like coming to London. I love performing it live because you just get to yell and scream. "Hold Back the Night" is one of the best vocals I've ever done. It was written by Bobby Bluebell of the Bluebells, and Dave Stewart found it for me to sing, and I don't think he could have found anything better.

"Dancing Lessons" I did with Wyclef Jean. That was very, very funny. He was kind of flirting with me for a moment until I had to say, "Don't be wasting time."

I was forced to put "The State I'm In" on *Faith and Courage* by the record company. I absolutely hate it. I didn't write it. It's not the type of song that's in my personality. Frank Merriman had always taught me never to sing a song that wasn't in my personality and here I bloody did. And I'm raging because I think it destroyed the album.

"The Lamb's Book of Life" was produced by She'kspere Briggs when I came to America to record some of the album. He didn't realize how depressed I was in Atlanta; he probably thought I was just the most boring bitch on earth (which I probably was) because all my complications back in London and Ireland were killing me.

But "The Lamb's Book of Life" is really the story of that awful period.

"If U Ever" is a song about my mother's death, an imaginary conversation between herself and myself. "Emma's Song" is about my relationship with my daughter's father, John Waters, whom I spoke about earlier, and "Kyrié Eléison," well, that was just for mischief—a Rastafied version of the first section of the Catholic Mass.

I had a great time making *Faith and Courage* because there were so many beautiful musicians and some of the most beautiful producers involved. As I've said, I can't remember many details because I was constantly stoned. It was a risk working with so many different creative minds, so the fact that it all came together is simply amazing to me. Apart from "The State I'm In," which I think is fucking terrible, I'm really, really proud of this record.

SEAN-NÓS NUA

FAITH AND COURAGE contains some of the best singing I ever did in my life. But the next album, *Sean-Nós Nua* — "old style new" in Gaelic — contains the *very* best singing that I ever did in my life.

It was a ghostly album, as these are many traditional Irish songs that no one can remember who wrote, so I feel they are like ghosts; you have to inhabit the character of these songs to bring them alive. *Sean-Nós Nua* was recorded in the most ghostly of places, and the strangest of events took place around the making of this album. We recorded in a very strange house in the countryside where there was what we call in Ireland a haunted tree; it was almost an evil tree. Not long after we made the album, the child of the house, a very small baby, died. It was all really sad. These are sad songs, of course, because nobody in Ireland ever writes a happy fucking song.

However, the songs and the album are very beautiful. It was produced by Dónal Lunny, as was my third child, Shane; if we had not made this album, we would not have made our beautiful son. I also again got Adrian Sherwood to work on this record, because nobody had ever reg-gaefied any of the old Irish songs.

"Peggy Gordon" is the most gorgeous of the songs; we deliberately set the key very high so that it would sound even more yearning. And no one ever sang a finer version of "The Moorlough Shore," "Molly

221

Malone," or "The Singing Bird." I know it's an awful sin and I'll probably burn in hell for boasting, but it's a very, very good album.

I think I'm still a good singer, but I will never be as good a singer as I was when I sang on *Faith and Courage* and *Sean-Nós Nua*. I was at the age where it was perfect.

Also, my relationship with Dónal Lunny, musically, was perfect. He had a great instinct as a producer; we had a brilliant working relationship, brilliant band, and brilliant record company. The whole thing worked really well. It's for a niche market, I guess. The record was number one in Ireland for a very long time.

Recording in Jamaica with Robbie Shakespeare (left) and Sly Dunbar (right)
COLLIN REID/AP PHOTO

THROW DOWN YOUR ARMS

IN 2005, I WAS LUCKY enough to go to Kingston, Jamaica, and record *Throw Down Your Arms* with Sly and Robbie (Sly Dunbar and Robbie Shakespeare) and the most incredible band on earth. I got to perform some of my favorite and most inspirational songs, which are all very male Rastafari numbers. I had the time of my life in Kingston with a friend of mine, who was very gay, for three weeks; at the time in Jamaica, you got ten years' hard labor for being gay. So I had to keep poking my friend's chin to make his mouth close every time he was staring at the lovely-looking men. And he was having an affair in our hotel room, which we were sharing, with one of the hotel's waiters, and the poor waiter kept thinking I was my friend's wife.

We recorded at Tuff Gong, and again, we made great music and smoked so much weed. Myself and Robbie Shakespeare fell quite in love and we had a big old affair. Later, when we toured for the album, myself and Robbie had a big bed in the back of the tour bus. We just loved those shows, but we were very in love with each other as well. Indeed, I loved everybody in the band; they were calling me Mommy 'cause I used to look after them a lot.

My favorite song on *Throw Down Your Arms* is "Prophet Has Arise," which was written by the great Jamaican reggae trio Israel Vibration; it gets me off the floor no matter how miserable I am. I later got to sing with Israel Vibration in Brixton Academy one night when my friend Benjamin Zephaniah was performing there and it was an incredibly moving experience. I got to hold the lead singer's hand and sing all those songs from Israel Vibration that I love. Did a lot of songs by the Jamaican roots musician Burning Spear, too, on *Throw Down Your Arms* because I love that man so much. I also learned an important lesson: never leave your weed in the dressing room when there is a band of Rastas there; it will be gone when you return.

When I made *Throw Down Your Arms*, I was a bit beaten down, to be honest. Bad stuff had been going on in my life. It was part of what led me into the spiritual arena. I also felt so strongly about making *Throw Down Your Arms*, I paid four hundred thousand dollars of my own money for the record's production. I was heading toward my next record, *Theology*, which is an album, believe it or not, that I had wanted to make since I was seven years old. *Throw Down Your Arms* was very much the precursor to *Theology*, which I also paid for personally. (I can't remember how much that one cost me.)

THEOLOGY

AROUND THE YEAR 2000, I went to college for a brief period to study theology. The books of the prophets were where my passion lay. We had the most beautiful teacher, a priest, who was able to bring God off the page when he was discussing the prophets. Particularly Jeremiah; he'd be going, "My poor people, my poor people," and his eyes would be streaming tears.

I wanted to do the same thing musically that he was doing when he was teaching, bringing God off the page. Let everyone see the humanity of God, the vulnerability, the moodiness, the emotionality.

One day I was reading the Song of Solomon quietly to myself while I was waiting for class to start and the teacher came in and bashed his finger on the book and said, "You should be writing songs about that." And so he inspired my record *Theology*; I'd really been thinking about it for a long time, but I didn't know how to realize it. There's a very fine line between corny and cool when it comes to writing religious songs, and I grew up in the 1970s with all these terrible charismatic Christian songs on the airwaves. So I didn't want to risk making that mistake.

Theology is the only album of mine I'm taking to the coffin. I love it. I took virtually all the lyrics from Scripture; I made one side just acoustic and the other with a full band because I couldn't make my mind up which one I liked best. Same songs, different covers. The way I worked was that I laid down on the floor huge pieces of paper, and I wrote down all of the lines that I loved that were in the Scriptures and decided to put them together and not change them but make them rhyme where I could. And there are some beautiful songs already written by God in the Scriptures.

"Something Beautiful" is the first song; it kind of declares my reason for wanting to make the record, and it describes a true story of a time that I stole a Bible (which I do think should be free). "Something Beautiful" is the one exception to the all-Scripture presentation, while "Out of the Depths" comes from one of the Psalms.

"Dark I Am Yet Lovely" is from the Song of Solomon. "If You Had a Vineyard" comes from the book of Isaiah. "Watcher of Men" is from the book of Job, which is very difficult to make rhyme and fit into three minutes.

For "Psalm 33," I made a different version of "The Rivers of Babylon" than people are used to hearing. And I love my version, not because of me but because it's beautiful, the words of it, the sentiment of people breaking their guitars because their tormentors require songs. It's not the most friendly of Psalms. There's an awful lot of baby-bashing and all.

"Whomsoever Dwells" is Psalm 91. I learned the Psalms in the Judaic way, where there are magical uses of the Psalms and how you use them with certain names of God. Psalm 91 is a bullet-stopper. The record company hassled me into putting "I Don't Know How to Love Him" on the album. I love that song, but it doesn't belong here. I also made a bad choice with "We People Who Are Darker Than Blue."

Theology was produced by my friend Graham Bolger and also Steve Cooney. Graham, at the time, had had a terrible accident (on my birthday, actually), in which he had slipped off his motorbike, crashed, and became a paraplegic. My place had a bungalow, and I invited him to stay there, which he did. Getting together and making this record was a good thing for him because he was going through such a terribly depressing time. Graham, Steve, and I were able to meet up every day and make the music; it let Graham see that life was still going to continue.

Graham is still a very good friend and somebody I love very much; we all had a really beautiful experience making *Theology*, another reason why it remains so very, very special.

I love performing these songs live. And as I said, if I go out in a coffin, it's the only record that I'm bringing with me to heaven in the hope that it will make up for what a complete piece of shit I am the rest of the time.

HOW ABOUT I BE ME

SEEING AS I WAS LOOKING after my kids, it took another couple of years to make my next record, *How About I Be Me*. I began to write songs from a different platform; I was writing about grief, misery, and my upbringing. I started to write just *songs*, some of which were inspired by movie scripts. For example, "Very Far from Home"—I had been sent a screenplay and I wrote a song for it. I didn't end up giving it to the movie, though. I just kept it for myself.

"Back Where You Belong" was a song for *The Water Horse*, the kids' film about the Loch Ness Monster starring Emily Watson. I gave it to them, and they used it, but I also used it for the record. We recorded it in my house in Monkstown in Dublin, and it was produced by Daniel Lanois. Daniel's a very sensitive character. The last time I saw him I was very worried about him—he was playing guitar at a gig with no plectrum and when he came off the stage, his fingers were cut to ribbons, literally deep cuts, bleeding and bleeding. I asked him what was wrong, and he told me his brother had died not long before. The poor man was in absolute tatters.

Daniel is very honest. We had once tried to record a version of John Lennon's "Mind Games" and I couldn't really sing that song. There are certain songs that I'm just not able to sing. Daniel was very honest with me about that. He's quite blunt, which I like about him. He doesn't kiss your ass, and that's a good producer quality. And he's very gentle about it. I've had producers who are terribly controlling because you're the artist or a woman (or both!); they want the full say, they want to interfere with your lyrics, things like that. But Daniel would never do that. He was always challenging, and I thank him very much for the work we did together.

"Take Off Your Shoes" is one of the songs that I'm proudest of. It's about the Holy Spirit talking to the pope and the Vatican around the time of all the church scandal reports. It is blasphemous by intent. I love the idea of a spirit singing, of me playing the character of a spirit. This really is the Frank Merriman/Stanislavski method of singing.

I also got to sing John Grant's "Queen of Denmark"; it's the greatest fun to perform live because it has the greatest chorus of any song on earth: "I don't know what it is you wanna want from me." The audiences go absolutely nuclear when they hear that chorus.

"Reason with Me" is a beautiful song about being a junkie. Not that I'm a junkie, but I'm a weed head. It's a song about being a weed head and being a fuckup. I used to pretend that none of the songs on this album were autobiographical because I couldn't be bothered talking about them. But they all are.

Except, that is, for "4th and Vine," the first track; it was definitely not autobiographical. It came about when John Reynolds was playing with a backing track, and I suddenly had a vision of women skipping along to their own weddings. So sometimes songs are just songs about nothing, and sometimes I'm writing about stuff I feel strongly about expressing.

The songwriting process for me is inside myself. I never sit down with a guitar and try to write a song. What happens is, the songs sing themselves to me bit by bit while I'm doing menial household tasks or while I'm walking around the street. One day, part of the song will sing itself to me. The following week, the next bit. The following week, the next bit. So I've never really sat down and tried to write a song as such. I just let them build themselves inside me like a little construction, and that's the point at which I would sit down with a guitar, when it's already finished inside myself.

The album cover for *How About I Be Me* became an issue. In Britain, I was disappointed that my manager and the record company felt that the beautiful painting of the little girl sitting in her nightgown on the Irish flag should not be used. (There's just a portrait of me on the EU edition.) But I didn't really have much choice except to allow it. It really was my first record that wasn't all about me, that wasn't all teenage angst or young-woman angst. Agreed, some of the songs may not be the happiest, but I was writing for other reasons about other things, other people, and other scenarios.

It marked a turning point, which I think began with *Sean-Nós Nua* and *Throw Down Your Arms* and *Theology*; they were stepping-stones for me to a place where I didn't have all this awful shit that I needed to get off my chest. So that's what this album represents for me.

I'M NOT BOSSY

MY EARLIER ALBUMS, by necessity, were diaries. *I'm Not Bossy,
I'm the Boss* I almost consider my first album. These were just three-min-
ute pop songs and love songs. Oddly, the first track on this album was
"How About I Be Me," which was the name of my previous album; it
was supposed to go there but was late for the masters. So I put it on *I'm
Not Bossy*, because I love it. It was originally a reggae tune; somebody
had given me the reggae backing track and I wrote it, but I ended up not
liking it reggae-style. "Dense Water Deeper Down" was a love song. Actually, it was about Brian Eno. "Kisses Like Mine" wasn't about anyone
in particular. I don't know really where it came from; I was just playing
the guitar and mucking around.

I got the backing track from John Reynolds, who produced the album, for "Your Green Jacket." It's a great song, all about something that
girls do—sniff fellows' clothes. If you love a man, you'd be sniffing his
shirt or you'd be sniffing his jacket. I'm sure guys do the same. Some
people think it's kind of stalkerish, but I don't think it's any more stalkerish than Adele's "Someone Like You," about "I had hoped you'd see
my face and that you'd be reminded that for me, it isn't over." With
"The Vishnu Room," I did what I'd never done before: wrote a long
song that revealed the kind of woman I can be. I'd never really written
vulnerable songs. I've heard other performers say the same thing. Amy

Winehouse, for example. She herself said she probably shouldn't have filmed her own funeral for the "Back to Black" video.

"Take Me to Church" is a song about songs and how what you write comes true so you've got to be very careful. The character in this song is writing songs about wanting this guy. Finally, she gets him—and she gets the crap scared out of her, as you can hear from the next song, "Where Have You Been?"

It's an interesting kind of journey, looking for romance, looking for love, falling in love, getting what you want, then finding out you want to run a million miles away. But it's not a sad thing. It's a pop record and they're love songs and they're beautiful and I'm really, really proud.

COMING SOON . . .

I THOUGHT THIS might be a chance to talk a bit about my next album, the one I'm working on now, in the summer of 2020. But let me back up a bit first.

Mr. X, a patient here at the Chicago Veterans Administration Hospital, isn't "difficult" at all, as the nurses had told me he was. He just wants internet. His eyes, whose lower rims have riverbeds in the middles from crying over his son who killed himself some years ago, are almost blind. So he has the hugest TV I've ever seen. It must be ninety-five inches, literally. He is attached by his nostrils to a large white oxygen machine which is on the floor by his chair, the tubing being long enough to allow him to stand up and walk around. He has emphysema. Lifetime of smoking. (I see I'm likely gonna go the same way.)

He tells me he isn't afraid of dying because he knows he's gonna see his son again and that he's been in the hospice for six weeks and didn't want to come in. He is full of life. One would never know he is dying. And I don't ask anyone, even him, how long he has.

He's ninety-two, from Syria, fought for America in the Korean War.

His wife died ten years ago. He shows me beautiful photos of them when they were young and going out to dances, all done up and looking so happy together. He has one surviving son, but he lives across the country so he can't be by his father's bedside.

So that's my job for about an hour every day or so for the time being.

He is part of a program called No Veteran Dies Alone. Companionship on the journey toward death for soldiers who have outlived their families or who just don't have family around for whatever reason.

I try to get internet for him, but fail. I don't know why the VA hospital has no Wi-Fi. So his TV may as well be a fish for all it's worth, and the only entertainment he has is my ugly face.

There's another old gentleman who waits for me every day in the foyer because I baffle him. He's a 'Nam vet. Also ninety-two. He doesn't know if I'm a boy or a girl because I regularly attend the hospital wearing a full Babe Ruth baseball outfit. And my head is, of course, shaved. This is a matter of astonishment to the gentleman. The morning after he established I'm female, he's waiting for me again. "So are you a lesbian?" he asks.

"No," I tell him.

"Then why would you cut all your hair off?" He's utterly bewildered but still waits every day for me because he never saw a heterosexual woman with no hair before. He doesn't realize I'm actually asexual. I don't bother enlightening him because he's already too mind-blown.

There's also a lady I look after, again ninety-two. She was a driver during World War II. She spends all day coloring pictures of Disney princesses. I buy her some fat markers with faces on them. The staff steal them from her right in front of me and I'm horrified.

When I push her in her wheelchair for her walks, she snaps out of being the Disney-coloring little girl back into being the soldier woman. With no words but with nods of her head, she shows me where snipers are positioned on the rooftops of the hospital. For real. Just in case.

So there's no internet but there are snipers. When there's no war. Go figure.

I'm lucky because none of my guys or gals die by the time I leave the job (which is voluntary) to return to Ireland. It's the best and most inspiring job I've ever had. I have a profound love for soldiers as a result.

So my next album is gonna be called *No Veteran Dies Alone* in honor of the program. I just wrote the title track. I'm gonna dedicate it to Mr. X. I'm also going to train in the autumn of 2020 to be a health-care assistant so I can get the diploma that allows me to companion the dying as my in-between-touring-and-recording job. It's been a dream of mine for years. Now I'm going to make it happen.

DAGGER THROUGH
MY HEART

MY FAVORITE COLLABORATION I've ever recorded was "Dagger Through My Heart," which I sang on a tribute record for Dolly Parton where she chose the singers. Why it's my favorite is because she sent me a lovely letter afterward thanking me and complimenting my interpretation of her song. I framed the letter and gave it to my stepmother, Viola, as a present. Because she and I both love Dolly.

I was remembering this last week as I was sitting on my porch on the seafront, watching the gate, as is my habit of a summer's very early morning. Then an old lady with short, white, windswept hair came walking her dog up my drive. She was waving an empty plastic water bottle and asking if she could fill it for her dog; her face was red, and she was upset. Her breath also seemed labored. The old lady said she was having a panic attack. So I sat her down and made her a cup of tea, and all the time the Dolly song singing itself away in my head.

She had a heart complaint and she'd heard bad news from someone on the seafront, so her heart was all over the place. She said that although she works in bereavement, when you know you're gonna lose someone close, it still breaks your heart. We sat a good hour. She was lovely. Apologizing all the time but not needing to. Not knowing she was the one doing me the favor.

She came back yesterday. Tidy-haired and "herself" again. So all the more I realized how upset she was the first time I saw her. I was cleaning the house from top to bottom. She said she was off to do the same and she gave me a beautiful white scarf. I think I love it as much as I loved the letter from Dolly. And I hope I see her again because she's a very special lady. I can't tell you her name except here's one clue: it's in a song I sang.

But she knows who she is and I'd like to thank her. Many weirdos wander up my drive. Rarely does an angel.

At the Dublin Special Olympics, 2003, with Muhammad Ali

THE GREATEST LOVE OF ALL

WHEN I WAS a very small child, my biggest hero and biggest inspiration was the boxer Muhammad Ali. My father got me up at least one night to watch one of his most famous fights, and I also saw a lot of footage of him on telly fighting, and I would watch anytime he was being interviewed on the news. I never liked watching the fighting. I didn't like the sight of Black men beating the crap out of each other for the entertainment and financial benefit of white men.

Also, as a victim, at the time, of child abuse, I hated watching the fighting, period. The idea of violence as entertainment is something which is abhorrent to me still, even though I did sing at Conor McGregor's fight. I held his mother's face to my breast so she wouldn't have to look at what her son was having done to him, never mind what he was doing to anyone else. Ali was well ahead of his time when it came to affirmations, and I loved him, as I'm sure all child-abuse survivors did, because we had similar self-esteem issues as African-American people had. We got there in a different way, but nevertheless, we were in a form of slavery, with a small *s*. It's arguable, I realize, whether one should apologize for using the word *slavery* to describe what it's like to be a survivor or a victim of child abuse, but, well, there it is.

Anyway, back to the point. Ali was able to reach across the whole world into the sitting rooms of Irish children and let us know that our parents were wrong. Jumping around yelling, "I'm the prettiest, I'm the greatest, I can do anything I want, I'm so beautiful"—these things were sins in our country not only for child-abuse survivors but for Catholic people. Because to be a good Catholic, you had to think you were a piece of shit. That was the idea. The less you thought of yourself, the more God would think of you. So Ali was able to reach into our sitting rooms and completely bust apart the theocracy and also bust apart the —I don't know what you would call it. The parent-ocracy? He let us see that, in fact, we were beautiful. We were salvageable, we were redeemable.

Not only that, but we were the greatest, and furthermore we were the prettiest too. He also showed us that we were going to make something of ourselves. That we were going to get up off the floor and transcend what happened to us. I recall an interview his daughter Laila, also a boxer, gave a few decades ago. Someone asked her, "Do you believe in God?" And what she answered—it nearly makes me weep—was "All I have to do to believe in God is look at my father." And that describes how I felt about her father, and I'm sure it described how the entire world felt about him too.

The most incredible experience I ever had, apart from having children, was meeting Muhammad Ali. Not only did I meet him, but myself and my eldest son, Jake, escorted him to the Special Olympics in Dublin in 2003. And this is how that happened.

Bon Jovi had played a show in Dublin, and the show was so loud that the neighbors complained, and you could hear the show where I lived, which was about twenty miles from the venue. And someone called me and asked if I would like to go to the after-party of the show, which I did, at a hotel called the Berkeley Court in Dublin, which was once where all the posh people used to stay.

I get to the party and start talking to Jon Bon Jovi's then wife, Heather, a very beautiful lady. And I happen to tell her how I love Muhammad Ali, and she says, "Oh my God, we're meeting Muhammad Ali tomorrow, because he and Nelson Mandela are hosting the Special

Olympics here." And I think nothing of it, and the next thing I start talking to her husband, to Jon Bon Jovi, who I don't know very well but who's a lovely guy. We end up chatting and he says, "Oh, yeah, we're meeting Muhammad Ali tomorrow." I don't dare say, *I'd love to meet him*. Instead, I say, "Oh my God, I'm going to die of jealousy right now, that guy is my biggest hero ever."

I think no more of it and I go home. Actually, after I leave Jon Bon Jovi, I go up the road to see Dónal Lunny and we end up making love, and I conceive my third child, which shouldn't have happened because I was nowhere near the middle of my cycle; in fact, I was menstruating. The child is eventually born on his father's birthday, two weeks early. This is a child who was meant to be born, and he actually has Ali in his name. Because this is the week in which I met Ali.

Sunday morning I get a phone call from somebody claiming to be Muhammad Ali's sports agent, and he asks if Jake and I want to come down to the Berkeley Court Hotel to meet Muhammad Ali. Now, you know, does a bear shit in the Vatican? Of course we'd like to meet Muhammad Ali. So I get my son out of bed, and we drive down there, and as soon as I get into the room, Muhammad Ali makes a kissing face . . . he wants me to give him a kiss. So that's enough to freak me out, I'm like, *Oh my God, this man is like my father*. Obviously he's not being sexual, it's platonic, so I give him the kiss and I'm like, *Oh my God, I've kissed the lips of Muhammad Ali*.

Ali, who by then was suffering through the latter stages of Parkinson's disease, starts playing jokes with Jake, which is just so sweet. He gets up out of his chair, and he's able to do this magic trick where he stands by the door and makes it look as if he's levitating by raising one of his feet and somehow magically being able to hide the other. Maybe he did levitate. And he also gave me a lovely present, which was a collection of Bible contradictions that he had put together himself. We're just sitting in the room and chatting with his wife and his family, then it's time to go. But just before we leave the room, his agent comes over to us and asks us if we would like to escort Mr. Ali to the Special Olympics. And the next thing you know, Jake and I are in an army car with a soldier. We end up escorting Muhammad Ali and sitting with him. And we're the only people sitting with him, just the only people helping him out during the night.

His family are around, obviously, but we are given the charge of Mr. Ali. I have to help him put on his jacket as he's walking down the corridor to sit in his place at Croke Park waiting for the Special Olympics to begin. As I'm putting on his jacket, I'm nearly crying. He's walking about an inch in front of me, he can't get the jacket on, and he's asking me for help. This is my father. I'm helping my father to put his jacket on. I can cry now even thinking about it.

Our attitude, myself and Jake's, God forgive us, was, like, fuck Nelson Mandela—everybody wanted to meet Mandela, of course, and everybody wanted to meet Ali too, but people got split along battle lines, almost. You were either Ali or Mandela, and we were totally Ali.

When we left to escort Ali back to his car, I saw the second-most-beautiful sight of my life—all the catering staff, young and old, crying, just weeping, to see Ali. Partly due to feeling sorry for him, which I hate, as nobody should feel sorry for Ali. His body may have been affected, but there was certainly nothing wrong with his mind. Regardless, I've never seen anything so incredible, literally every space in the catering window and doorway filled with faces watching to see such a holy man walk through the place.

After that night, I kept in touch for a short while with Ali's agent, who in fact I was very interested in getting into bed with as well (I really was ovulating that week). But luckily, he had a friend staying with him, so that never happened. I did give him a lion Rasta ring.

Oh, I forgot to tell you. There was a moment during the backstage time that Ali drew a beautiful picture on a tablecloth. It was a huge ship sailing through a valley. On the other side of the tablecloth, he drew one of his fights, tiny. Me and the soldier are looking at each other in the dressing room, saying, "You're going down"; "No, you're fucking going down"; "No, you're fucking going down." Because we were bargaining over which one of us was going to get it. Of course I won. Ali signed it for me, and he gave it to me, and I gave it about a year ago to my son Jake, because he's thirty-two now and I wanted to wait until he was old enough to look after it.

It was all magical, and I could never have imagined it would happen in my life. I've been a very lucky person in that every dream I've ever had has come true. But more than that, dreams that I never even dared to dream came true. So yes, and if not for that week, and if not for the fact that my son's father was situated up the road, and thank God Ali's sports agent had somebody staying with him, my third son would not have been born. My son is called Nevi'im Nesta Ali Shane. *Nevi'im* is the Hebrew word for the books of the prophets. I knew that he was going to be semi-fatherless, so I wanted the prophets to be his father, his male guides.

Nesta is the actual name of Bob Marley. Ali is obviously my chosen godfather, along with Dylan, and Shane is after my friend Shane MacGowan, the musician. So quite the week that was, and I have to thank Muhammad Ali for the existence of my son, and yes, it was the most incredible experience of my entire life (apart from having babies, obviously).

LOU REED

THE ONLY OTHER TIME I remember being starstruck was when I met Lou Reed, a person I didn't realize I loved so much until I met him. I had fallen in love with his album *New York*, especially the track called "Busload of Faith," and I had listened to it a lot. And suddenly there I am in Carnegie Hall and I'm booked to sing at Roger Daltrey's fiftieth-birthday show. And in those days, I used to be quite naughty and I would ask people if I could sing backing vocals with them.

So I put the word around that if at all possible I would love to sing some backing vocals with Lou Reed. And the next thing I knew, Lou Reed came into my dressing room and started talking to me; I could tell that he thought I was cheeky for asking if I could sing backup vocals. But when he said that yes, I could, all I could see was his mouth moving. I couldn't hear what he was saying anymore; it all came out like a *whirl, whirl, whirl* sound, as if I were on an acid trip. His face and mouth moving, but I couldn't understand anything he was saying. It was like having a panic attack. I had to get my friend Doodles, who was also visiting backstage, to hold my hand for half an hour after he left. I did do the backing vocals for Lou, though I can't remember even what songs because I was not on planet Earth, I was in heaven somewhere. And then I had a beautiful experience with the same beautiful man not long after.

I was booked to do a show in London called *The White Room* and the idea of it is that perhaps six or seven bands are set up in a circle and each one plays a couple of songs and then the next one plays a couple and so on. When I arrived for the dress rehearsal, everybody turned their back on me, because the fashion was to treat me like a crazy person, a pariah, because of what I did on *SNL*. So apart from my own band, nobody would have anything to do with me. Still, everybody was as excited as me about the fact that Lou Reed was on the show.

So Lou Reed, when he comes to the dress rehearsal, makes a huge point of ignoring absolutely everybody in the room except me. He makes it his business to find me, hangs on to me. He hugs me demonstratively warmly as if we know each other really well. It was a really sweet thing to do because he didn't have to do that, and it changed the way everybody in there reacted to me. I began to get treated with a little bit of respect as I did my rehearsal and my performance. I've had a very soft spot in my heart for Mr. Lou Reed ever since and I think about him quite a lot.

SOME LESSONS
AND TRUE TALES

I LOVE PERFORMING more than anything else on this planet. Apart from my children, of course. And one of the things I think about as I get set to start another tour (when the pandemic ends) is how bizarre and sometimes perilous celebrity can be.

Years ago, we played a show in Las Vegas, I believe it was at the Hard Rock Café. Johnny Depp was at the show and afterward he came backstage. His visit came at a moment when we had been on tour so long, we'd lost our minds slightly.

Caroline Dale, my cello player, had a bag that looked like a child's stuffed sheep. We called the sheep Shaun. It had been everywhere on tour with us, and it became our mascot. That night in Vegas, we decided we would wed this sheep to some other cuddly animal that had made its way into our entourage. It was an elaborate ceremony and Johnny Depp had to stand and watch us go through this forty-minute-long wedding.

I never saw him again, needless to say. Actually, that's not true. I met him recently at Shane MacGowan's sixtieth-birthday party, and he volunteered, very politely, that in fact he had had lots of fun that night. I'm sure he just thought we were mental. Coincidentally or not, this all occurred while Johnny was in Vegas playing Hunter S. Thompson in the movie of *Fear and Loathing in Las Vegas*.

Speaking of odd encounters, or odd non-encounters, the story that I met John F. Kennedy Jr. at some posh dinner and that he offered me his phone number and I ripped it up is absolutely untrue. Great anecdote, but I never even met the man. I would've leaped on him like a monkey had I met him, the same as any other woman would. Yes, I would have had to be gay to turn that number down.

There have also been some misconceptions out there about me and Anthony Kiedis of the Red Hot Chili Peppers. In his memoir *Scar Tissue*, he describes us kissing. It never happened.

He says we had some type of romantic relationship. Only in his mind.

We hung around together and he's a very nice gentleman; I even remember him helping me bring my son to the hospital once. I got annoyed when he wanted to take it further. God help him. He had the O'Connor temper unleashed on him not because he tried to kiss me but because he intimated that he would like to, you know, as it were, stoke the fire. He confused me completely with some other bull chick. That never happened.

MR. BIGSTUFF

IT ISN'T JUST THE RUMORS that swirl when you find yourself a celebrity that's disturbing, it is the danger of how some people are willing to hurt you for profit.

A so-called friend found a photo of me on my iPad that I'd taken of myself and texted to a husband who is unusually fond of pocket billiards. In it, I'm wearing nothing but a very skimpy French maid–looking outfit, with my ass all on show.

It's lucky that I own the photo's copyright because my so-called friend gave the photo to some knucklehead who is now calling up Irish newspapers trying to sell it to them. A reporter I know called to give me a heads-up (pardon the pun).

I'm determined to prevent any publication so I take that knucklehead's number from my reporter friend and I text him claiming to be a reporter from an English tabloid that wants to buy the photo. He falls for it. And I arrange to meet him at a gas station maybe five miles from my home. I go there early, wearing a long brown wig. And I sit low down in my car for about twenty minutes until I can identify which car he is in. Turns out he's parked right beside me.

I walk into the store pretending to buy something. And as I walk back, I stop at his car and very ostentatiously take a photo of his license plate.

He's baffled. Staring at me wondering, *What's this woman up to?* By the time I'm back in my car and strapped in, it's dawned on him. And he speeds off onto the highway. And I follow him in my seven-seater mom car speeding after him for about three miles. There's a proper car chase until he turns left in his swifter vehicle. Goes down a back country lane and manages to hide himself. He knows the area well. It's where he lives.

I call him. He's shitting himself. I inform him I own the copyright. He refuses to admit my so-called friend gave it to him. But she did; she's the only one who's been at my iPad.

He's very sorry. So he says. And he will dump the photo. I never hear another word about it. And I never see that so-called friend again. Ain't the first time she's used me for money. It makes me very sad. She's always stealing stuff from me. So are other people. It would actually break my heart if it weren't broken already.

JAKE, ROISIN, SHANE,
AND YESHUA

I HAVE FOUR CHILDREN by four different fathers, only one of whom I married, and I married three other men, none of whom are the fathers of my children.

I can honestly say that the father of my first child and the father of my last child are my best friends in this world. However, with the fathers of the two children in the middle, we would indeed cross the road if we saw each other.

As I wrote earlier, my first child, Jake, was a very pleasant surprise, conceived because of the fact that a girlfriend of mine told me that day fourteen of one's cycle is the safest, and so I did not make love with his father until day fourteen, which took place in some country town in England while a Madonna concert was playing on the television.

I would say that Jake suffered some due to the fact that I was so young when I had him and that I also had suddenly become extraordinarily successful in the music business—three weeks before he was born was the release of my first album. At age twenty, I would not say I understood the concept of selflessness the way one ought to when one becomes a parent.

I know that I was a good mother when it came to Jake and my three other children, but it's difficult to be a very good mother when you are a touring musician. I was affectionate and loving, but I was away a lot, and even when I was home, I was rather like an automaton, tired and worn out and also very frightened that I might be like my own mother; I always made sure I had a nanny because I was afraid I might turn out like her. At the end of the day, this might have bothered Jake. I think it was read mistakenly as some part of me not caring, but I wanted to make sure that my children would never have to go through what I went through; if I were in some type of mood, I could go upstairs or I could leave the house, and my children wouldn't have to deal with that.

Having Jake while I was very young had benefits, especially in that we were the best of friends. As he grew older, we became closer. We were often more like friends than mother and son, which I suppose is not necessarily always a good thing, but we had a very beautiful relationship.

My cooking has always been a problem for my children. I am not a good cook. In fact, that is an understatement. One could demolish a house or break a window with anything that I cook. Consequently, Jake became a good cook at a very young age and he now works as a head chef in a restaurant in Dublin; he has an enormous work ethic of which I'm extremely proud. This is a very, very hardworking young man.

Jake now has two children of his own, a daughter, Naime, and a son, Louie, so I am a grandmother to two beautiful kids currently aged one and three.

When I was ill two or three years ago, it was very difficult for Jake to be around me. But I'm happy to say we are very good friends again and I love that child with all my soul, just as I love all my children. In fact, I secretly tell each of them that they're my favorite, but I also tell them not to tell their siblings I said that. Every time I see any of them, I go, "You're my best. Don't tell the others."

My daughter, Roisin, was not a surprise; she was planned. Her father is a gentleman by the name of John Waters, a journalist who used to write for the *Irish Times* in Ireland. We met so he could interview me about my controversial song "Famine," which was on the album *Universal Mother*.

I would not say that we fell in love; we did not. I had just had a miscarriage. We got on very well, and agreed to have a child with each other with the understanding that we would not be together. So we conceived Roisin and had an arrangement whereby she spent half the time with her father and half her time with me. While I have no relationship with John, he has been a fantastic father, an absolutely wonderful father.

I'm very proud of Roisin, especially because she was so well behaved growing up; I can't tell you any mischievous stories. But what I can tell you is that she has a guardian angel. Not only have I seen this guardian angel, many of her friends have seen this little angel too.

I didn't believe her friends who told me they saw this little girl angel and I didn't believe a boyfriend of mine when he told me he'd seen this little red-haired girl too. At least not until one morning when I was pregnant with my third child, Shane, and I was sleeping in the bed with Roisin. I woke up and there the angel was, sitting on top of Roisin with her head in her hands as if she were just bored and waiting for her to wake up. I saw this little red-haired girl, wearing a red and white sweatshirt.

It was so *not* scary that I went straight back to sleep. When I woke up again about an hour later, the little girl was still sitting on top of Roisin. I went back to sleep again and when I woke up the next time, the little girl was gone. But a week later, I was berating Roisin over the state of her bedroom in what I call the futility room instead of the utility room, and a huge, four-liter bottle of water chucked itself off the countertop and onto the floor—clearly the guardian angel wasn't very happy with me being mad at Roisin.

On Roisin's second birthday, she came rushing toward the table on which there was a carving knife with its pointed edge directly at her eye level. When she was a millimeter away from the knife, it lifted itself up into the air and moved to the left to get away from her face, obviously the work of her guardian angel. I have neither seen nor heard guardian angels around my other children, but I presume they are there. However, Roisin's guardian angel is such a strong character that she makes herself visible.

Interestingly, like Jake, Roisin also turned out to be a chef, but in Roisin's case, she is a pastry chef. She trained in Paris and is now working in Ireland. She has tiny, dainty hands. She was always able to make the teeniest Play-Doh creatures with those delicate fingers of hers, and now she makes beautiful pastries and vegan cookies.

I just think it's hilarious that so far two of my kids have become great cooks. I do notice, however, that they do not send their mother any care packages full of food. Since I have mild anorexia, I consider starving, but I would still like some of Roisin's pastries to arrive in a box, so I hope that after she reads this book, one will.

You don't want to cross Roisin. And the only way you will cross Roisin is if you are a bigot. Roisin will get up and walk away from you. She does not have her mother's temper, thanks be to God, so she will turn her back on you and be quiet and not bother speaking to you again. I admire her for her ability to walk away from an argument; I am inclined to run right toward one. And I aspire to be more like my daughter in that respect.

Roisin is now happily married to a lovely man she calls Poldy. He's exactly like Roisin's brother Jake, which is very sweet. Roisin and Jake have an absolutely beautiful relationship and always have had one; they will literally sit on each other's knees, hug, and cuddle. I don't believe they've ever had a row. If you mess with Roisin, you're going to have to deal with Jake, and believe you me, that's not something you want to try.

Shane is my third child, born in 2004. He was a surprise. His father was married at the time, so there was great controversy around the fact that I was pregnant.

I remain very fond of the child's father, Dónal Lunny, although we are not close. Things became very difficult for Shane and for me.

Shane is an extremely special character, very, very psychic and very,

very spiritualized. When he was three, he asked me one day, "Were you in an earthquake when I was inside your tummy?" At first I said no because I forgot that I had been. When he was two weeks in my belly—I didn't even know I was pregnant—I was on holiday in Malta, and there was an earthquake. I never thought about it again, I never mentioned it. I never told the child; I don't think I even told anyone else. Yet this three-year-old child was able to tell me I was in fact in an earthquake, and I don't know how he knew this.

Another time he was in his bath, and he asked me, "Did you ever meet God?" And I said, well, maybe I did, some kind of magical things happened to me, and maybe I met God in certain ways. The child tut-tutted at me as the water was leaving the bath and said, "That's not how you meet God," he told me. "You have to make your dreams come true."

Shane was assessed at age eight and declared a genius. I was told that he had the learning ability, the vocabulary, and the mathematical reasoning of a sixteen-year-old. He began to study science at a college with the adults in Dublin, but he didn't enjoy going there, so it didn't last long.

He reminds me very much of Clint Eastwood. He could get himself into all kind of trouble, but because he is so calm and so sweet and so genuinely charming, he manages to sail through things without them affecting him terribly badly, and I admire him for that.

I know it is said that children like Shane can be difficult and challenging. But it is actually easy for me, because I'm an unusual kind of mother. Shane is not a square peg to be shoved into a round hole. He is the child who is most like me, I believe, to look at and by his nature —although he is of course the version of me with logic and reason. As Jack Nicholson might say, he is a very cool customer, Shane.

I suspect this child is going to go into some type of work that involves helping people; he may turn out to be a very good chef. He would rather starve to death than eat anything I make. He's the type of cook who doesn't need a recipe and just throws everything into the pot and the pan, and it turns out great. Another testament to my terrible, terrible cooking, although it does seem I do cook me a good baby.

Yeshua was planned. He was born, I would say, two weeks early, on December 19, 2006. While I was pregnant with him, interestingly, the only craving I had was silence. With my other children, the cravings were types of food—in Jake's case, sausages and kiwifruit; in Roisin's case, lime pickles; and in Shane's case, fish pie. All Yeshua wanted was silence.

I used to have to put myself in a dark room and just sit there very, very silent. And it turns out Yeshua is a very silent person. His father, Frank Bonadio, has a daughter named Claire who also has the same silence, and my grandmother had a great silence around her. Yeshua is very much the same.

He loves his own space and likes to be alone. An extraordinarily creative human being, he is definitely the child who I think will become a singer—he has a phenomenal voice, a phenomenal musical talent. He plays the piano so well that you would think a record was playing.

I am rarely speechless, but when I hear him play piano and when I hear him singing, I cannot speak for ten minutes. As soon as he starts performing, I'm out of the picture. Yeshua is going to blow me off the stage and out of the water. So I'm deliberately being very nice to him (and so is the rest of the family) because we reckon he's going to be a millionaire by the time he's twenty and we want to make sure he's good to us.

He's turned into a teenager obsessed with superheroes and Harry Potter. If you meet him, all he will talk about is which superhero he would like to be and which superpower he would like to have. He's genuinely upset that he doesn't have a superpower. Although I'm always telling him he does, in fact, have a superpower: his large empathetic heart and the amount of love he has for people. Of course, he scoffs at me, saying, "You can't save the universe with a large empathetic heart." I disagree.

Yeshua is one of the funniest people I've ever met, with a laugh that makes everybody else laugh, even if you don't know what he's laughing at, because he literally cry-laughs and giggles.

Something I'm finding very sweet these days is that he's turning into a carbon copy of his father. He even sits exactly as his father sits. And I have to say, his father is the best father that I've ever encountered. And Lord knows, Father's Day is a busy day in my house. In fact, it's quite the revolving door.

People always want to know why I have four children with four different men. I tell them it just happened that way. It wasn't something I planned, but I didn't feel like I had to get married for the sake of having a child. Although I did marry my first child's father, we were, as I wrote, more like brother and sister. (That's why that relationship did not work out; I couldn't compute how one might make love with one's brother.)

John Reynolds and I got married because we thought we should—or, I should say, because I thought we should, because we had a child together. That is not a mistake I was prepared to make again. So when I found myself pregnant by surprise with Shane, I was in love with Shane, although I didn't want to be with his father. The same was the case with Roisin. In Yeshua's case, myself and Frank were together five years, and we still remain the best of friends and we live three hundred feet from each other so the child can come and go as he pleases. I didn't set out to be unusual or independent. These were four babies that I wanted.

I did have quite a funny time on tour a number of years ago when I had to explain to a German customs man calling from the Munich airport why my four children had four different surnames. The man was worried that I was child-trafficking. I was on the phone with him in my hotel, and my children were being brought to visit me by their male nanny, who also had a different surname. It took about twenty minutes to explain to the customs agent what the story was. Nothing made sense to him until I said, "Look, I was a bit of a slut." And then he said, "Oh, okay." And that was that. But I was joking.

Interesting little footnote: One night years ago my own father came to visit me and told me that he was almost jealous of the way I lived my life with regard to having children, not feeling like I had to get married and live the way a man might like to live. In short, while it's okay in society for men to have children with different women, sometimes women get looked down upon for having four children with four different men or, really, any amount of children with different men.

I have never actually been looked down upon for that, nor have I ever experienced any stigma from it. All I have experienced is my poor daddy saying he wished he could have lived his life the way I live mine.

If I have no other purpose in this life other than to put these four children on this earth, well, that's enough for me to feel I did something useful in this world. I am not just saying that because they are my children. They are absolutely unusual, intelligent, loving, compassionate, spiritually advanced, funny, worthwhile, hardworking human beings, and I couldn't be prouder.

THE WIZARD OF OZ

THE REASON I HAVEN'T WRITTEN much about what happened between 1992 and 2015 is that in August 2015, after I'd written the first part of this book, I had an open-surgery radical hysterectomy in Ireland followed by a total breakdown.

I had gotten as far as the *Saturday Night Live* story, but I did not write anything else for the four years it took me to recover from the breakdown, and by the time I'd recovered, I was unable to remember anything much that took place before it.

As part of my recovery journey, I spent the guts of 2016 and 2017 in different parts of America because the mental-health-care system in Ireland was failing me (for example, I wasn't offered any hormone replacement therapy) and because no one who knew me wanted anything to do with me; I was so out of my mind that they were all terrified of me. No one had explained to them or me that the loss of one's ovaries would result in what is called surgical menopause, which is menopause times ten thousand, and that I might become very unstable.

In America they tell your family these things, and they tell you, the patient. In America the psych hospitals recognize you've just had your entire womanhood reamed out. And they get you on hormone replacement. There was none of that in Ireland. I left the hospital in Dublin after the hysterectomy with no information, nothing but a bottle of Tylenol and a follow-up appointment to which I dared not go.

I'd had to have the surgery because I had chronic endometriosis. I didn't actually need my ovaries taken out too. The doctor just decided he "might as well" whip them out. If he'd left them you'd have a lot more information about 1992 to 2015. But maybe it's good to forget stuff. There was so much pain, after all, involved with being a pariah for decades after *SNL*.

Not that I would change any of it. Some things are worth being a pariah for.

In America in 2016 I stayed a few days with the one person I knew who might have an available floor. He then put me with a lovely family he knew, the Walkers. Which I was glad about because I didn't like the way he treated his wife; he dealt with her like she was dirt. (When I left, I should have taken her with me.)

While staying with the Walkers, who lived in a tree-lined suburb of Chicago called Wilmette, I went to lots of psych appointments and had lots of counseling. Matt Walker is Morrissey's drummer. His wife is Charlotte. And they are the people I owe my life to because if not for them having me live with them and if not for Charlotte bringing me to the doctor and the therapy appointments and staying around with me, I wouldn't be here tonight writing. Without her at that time I could not walk.

But we had so much fun. She is dark-humored like myself. And so is her mother, who is in her nineties, the most beautiful long-dark-haired lady you've ever seen. She had tons of lovers when she was young. And she is really crude. You can have a great joke with her. I have a nickname for her that is so rude I won't write it. But it used to make her cry-laugh. Because it was so true.

But I was staying in the Walkers' daughter's room, and she came back from college, so it was time to get my own place. I moved into a motel in nearby Waukegan.

I was very lonely. But I also enjoyed the fact that at the motel I could smoke. And I loved the massive Walmart right opposite the motel where I would buy useless material things to try to feel something like excitement and to make my room look more like a home.

At some point I bought some weed that made me feel sick, so I decided to give up the weed and went out to San Francisco to a rehab recommended by someone my therapist knew. I stayed there three months. Then I went back to Ireland for like a week but still no one wanted to know me. So I went back to America, to New Jersey, and my manager sorted me an apartment in the same building as him. But I was so suicidal I couldn't stay in it for more than a day or so and I had to keep going to hospital.

In the final of three visits to Englewood Hospital, which took place after scores of visits to Hackensack University Medical Center, and after I parted with my manager, and after I moved into a motel somewhere in New Jersey and got a kidney stone and made a video appeal on Facebook for someone to come help me, a call comes through for me on the ward from Dr. Phil. I'm thinking maybe it's my Cinderella moment.

He wants to help me. Says his researcher found me via my immigration lawyer, Michael Wildes, because his photo and name had been on my Facebook page.

As Phil is introducing himself on the phone, a wine-shirted blond-haired health-care assistant aged about eighteen with the palest skin you can imagine is supervising me, as is the case with all suicidal patients. I was never in any hospital in America that one kind lady wasn't with me all day and another all night, and it's those ladies who made me want to be a health-care assistant myself because the talking and giggling with them was more healing than any medicine or therapy. Knowing they'd be there while I was sleeping was the closest I've ever felt to being mothered. So it wasn't oppressive being watched; it was loving.

Anyway, her skin was so white it was like paper, so when a vicious crazy lady walked by and threw half a cup of boiling tea on the girl's arm and no one came to help her, I felt I had to put the phone down. I made a fuss at the desk that she'd been ignored, in the midst of which I get a

267

note slipped to me by a nurse. It's from the man who was my doctor at Hackensack. He's heard about Dr. Phil and he agrees with the doctor at Englewood that it would not be healthy to do the show.

I think they're both nuts. He's Dr. fuckin' Phil. He can fix anyone. And they haven't exactly got a clue either! So what have I got to lose?

Of course, I'm the crazy one. But sadly, they cannot legally prevent me from leaving the hospital (which would have been in my best interests), and I insist on accepting Phil's call back, which comes about ten minutes after the old lady throws the tea.

It's important you understand how desperate for a cigarette one is after a few days and nights in any American psych ward. It's not like Ireland, where the only good thing is they let you smoke. In America, there's fuck-all for you but a nicotine patch. And there's no outdoor area. So after a week, you're losing your mind even more than you already were, and so my insistence on abandoning all reason and going to Dr. Phil was in huge part based on my desire to get outside and smoke. And furthermore, smoke some weed. Which was also agony to be without at the time. Phil was offering me an eight-hour car ride to a treatment facility he had recommended to some of his guests in America's South. My sneaky addict mind knew that was hours of weed and cigarettes. And, yes, sir, it was, all the way.

I'd been introduced to a new lady manager while at the hospital and we went with the driver and two-man film crew Phil had sent to my abandoned apartment to meet the weed man, then I climbed into the big black van, kissed my manager goodbye, and sailed off into the night, certain that this time I'd be cured. I don't mean of smoking, I mean of being angry and suicidal and too full of pain to function outside a hospital. I had been praying that God would send Himself to help me in the form of a human being. And I really thought the one God had sent was Dr. Phil. I thought he was literally the answer to my prayers. But I should have known he was batting for the other team. Because he wasn't spiritually honest. On Jimmy Fallon's show he was asked how he and I got together. "She contacted me," he said. Not true. If he had told the truth, Jimmy might have accused him of exploiting someone while she was very fragile.

So after eight hours of driving and smoking and talking we got to this trauma-treatment center in the beautiful ass end of Nowhere. The doctors in New Jersey had said (rightly, it transpired) that a trauma treatment would be dangerous because I was so vulnerable. But no one had listened. First bullshit is the people at the center want to take my iPad. They might as well have tried to take my lungs. I ran them round the property in the black of night, then shoved it down my pants and hid in bushes while two women roamed around the grounds in a golf cart, searching for me and it. In the end, I gave in and they got it. And in protest, I wouldn't take any of my possessions into my room. I told them they could keep everything else I had if they were taking my iPad. Because it's cruel to just take a person's crutch and leave them sitting in their shit with no comfort or distraction for twenty-four hours a day. Especially if their shit happens to be a load of trauma. So I went overnight from having some comfort to zero comfort. And I hated the ladies for it. But only for a day. Because it transpired they were lovely, both of them.

I meet the psychiatrist at the trunk of his car as I'm stomping back from the garden toward my room. He offers me a fig bar. What the fuck does a rocker want a fig bar for? Is he crazier than me? I tell him, "No, thank you, fig bars are for hippies." I can see we ain't gonna be getting along at all.

It's late by the time all is settled for the night. I get to bed about one a.m. Dr. Phil's show people are coming in the morning, because the condition upon which Phil helped me was that I had to do the show. And I had to do it before I had any treatments at this place where he had referred me. That way you don't get to complain on camera afterward about how badly you've been exploited and how reckless your so-called medical care seemed at the place he recommends.

I mean, I'm not even sure anyone on my treatment team sought my medical records from any hospitals I'd been in. Including Englewood, from whence he'd plucked me. So they didn't seem to know if I should be subjected to even one hour a week of individual trauma therapy, never mind nine hours a day. I felt brutalized. Making me even more unwell.

So anyway, now I'm sitting in front of Dr. Phil, ready to shoot the show. Full of hopes and dreams. First thing he says is he's here because my fans wrote to him after my Facebook video and asked him to help me. He waves a vast folder he claims is full of their e-mailed requests. All full of love and support for me. I ask if I can keep the folder and its contents. He says yes but forgets to give it to me. He tells me how lucky I am now, that because this place I'm in is so opulent et cetera, it's gotta be the best.

He makes me tell him my story on camera. I trust him because I'm vulnerable. And I want to live. So I go ahead and let it all hang out. I cry like a baby. He even makes me speak to my mother. The things "little Sinéad" might want to say. Which I do. Because I think he's helping me. Oh, and also because I'm given the vibe before shooting begins that my being on the show while I'm so fragile is "brave" and "will help others." He goes on about some big producer he knows. Swears this guy is gonna call me and we're gonna make records. When we're filming a final walk around the property, he tells me he was recently at a meeting attended by Steve Bannon. And that the Trump people had actually discussed at that meeting the idea of MAGA being MAWA. Make America White Again. He acted all disgusted when telling me.

But I figured if he was really that disgusted, he'd be telling the world. That would be spiritual honesty. To risk losing all you have to save the vulnerable. To risk being called crazy and being a pariah. No. He didn't have the balls.

Off he flew in his chopper and I never saw him again.

The following day me and the psychiatrist had a disagreement. He accused me (falsely) of wanting to be treated like a rock star because I'd forgotten to sign out when I was going for smokes.

I was insulted because I would never actually want to be treated differently than anyone else in a treatment facility. And it showed me his fig bars had gone to his brain.

I was hurt. But I never said a word. I just quietly left his office and went to my room.

Apparently he assumed I was in a rage and he went running off up a hill to get away in case I came after him. That just made me angry when I hadn't been angry. The fucking shrink is a fig-eating pussy and you can't even cry around him or he'll fall to pieces. Jesus Christ. I told them not to put me back in a room with him for fear I'd hit him. So Phil was called and he duly called me. I told him my concerns about the fig-eater and the attentiveness of the rest of the staff. I told him also I didn't think I could be fixed (which I still think).

"I don't fail," Dr. Phil said. And warned me not to be battering the shrink.

Things go from bad to worse each time I make a formal complaint about the facility's crew. Or about the other suicidal girl Phil sent them after a show, sobbing to me about not getting the care she felt she needed although she said she was having urges. I'm eventually put out of the main facility to live on my own in a vast, empty, rather grand house that was on the grounds. I'm not allowed into the main house. Which makes me very angry. As do the nine hours of trauma therapy every day. (One day, in the middle of a marathon trauma-therapy session, in walks one of the male staff in charge of legal and accounting. He handed me a contract he wished me to sign. Saying if I recorded anything—all clients did as part of their treatment—with the music therapist, the recordings would be owned by the treatment center. Needless to say, I didn't sign and it's disgusting that anyone would tramp into someone's therapy session for any reason, never mind to let that person know you wanted to take advantage of her.)

· · ·

So I finally lose my shit one night, shouting my head off all over the place, and cops are called because I've said I'm suicidal. I'm taken to the local hospital where they assess that I'm not actually suicidal but traumatized. They advise me not to return to the treatment center. And the cops then very kindly find me a motel and take me there.

In the morning, inside my bag, I find the key to the big house I'd stayed alone in at the treatment center. And stupidly decide to bring it back. I call the only cabdriver in town. He tells me he has a bullet in his head from the Korean War and that all the ladies of the town want him. As we drive down the road, I see a beautiful graveyard on our left. White statues and carvings. All giant religious symbols and flowers.

On the right side of the road, opposite this, is what looks like an animal graveyard. Maybe a hundred black stones the size of grapefruits are in the ground but there are no discernible graves. The grounds are unkempt, the grass uncut. I ask my driver if it's an animal graveyard. "No," he says. "That's for the Black people but I don't hang out with them much." I feel my heart rip in two. And now I understand why the one Black lady who works at the center was so astonished it was her shoulder I chose to cry on when things got too much. She'd been shocked the first time it happened and thanked me as if it were an honor.

I go to give the key back and I get talked into going to LA to another treatment center. Which I agree to and am flown there and dumped. I hear nothing from Phil, although I've been told he's underwriting my stay. After three weeks, one of the staff, in a temper, informs me I'm in fact being put up for nothing by the center and that what I'd heard at my first facility wasn't the case. No surprises there. I pack up and leave. And I have never heard from any of them since.

I wrote a song about all this in 2018. It's called "Milestones" and will be on my next album, though a demo of it is already out on YouTube. And no, it doesn't mention fig bars.

A scripture painting

COURTESY OF THE AUTHOR

FORWARD AND NOW

IN ISLAM, WE BELIEVE that in heaven it's always night. I hope so. And I hope if there's a heaven, I qualify (if there's such a situation as not qualifying). I have a hard time believing God would be cruel. But just in case I deserve otherwise, I hope the fact I've sung will make little of my sins, which are ugly and legion.

I love fire. I hope there are fires in heaven. Fire makes me strong when I am unable.

I also love nighttime best because that's what fire is for. And if my nighttime has no fire in it, nor my dark morning? I am bereft. Naked, even. As I would be without my hijab.

I have worn it since October 2018 (not the same one, and, yes, I've washed it so my head doesn't smell like a foot) when I reverted. We say *revert* because Islam feels like home. That's what it was like for me as a person who had studied theology since I was a child. Like coming home. I searched all my life, through every book and every song, and for some reason I left Islam until last. Despite the fact I played the call to prayer before every show for years, I'd never sat down to study it.

I have a hobby I haven't spoken about. I paint Scriptures. Been doing it a long time. I usually give them to people but lately I don't because I've noticed I end up falling out with almost anyone I give one to.

When I shuffle off this mortal coil, I want every person to whom I gave a painting to gather in one place and have an exhibition. These people have never met. They are from all walks of life. I'd like them to meet if they haven't trashed the paintings. And even if they have.

I switched to drawing because every painting took me a month and I'd end up in a hospital from not eating. Painting was like an addiction. I use markers now. And gold-leaf paint. Easier. Same result. It's my way of praying. So I sat down in the middle of some night that October to paint the call to prayer. Praying in another language is like singing. You have to know what you're saying. So I had the English and the Arabic versions and wished to paint the Arabic. I got so blown away by what *La ilaha illallah* means ("There is no God but God") and how it felt in my mouth to say it, the mathematics of it. That was it, I was home. The language and intelligence of the call to prayer led me to listen to the Koran. I was home. I'd been a Muslim all my life and never realized it. The call to prayer is the most mathematically intelligent song ever written.

Idolatry (loving something or someone more than God) is anything you love so much you think you'd die without it. Or you'd want to die without it. Could be a person, place, or thing. You won't know until God decides to show you. But show you He will. A golden calf of your own. And you'll be stunned because you thought you were a true believer.

In heaven, they say it's paradise. Nighttime paradise. Cool and calm. Gardens with rivers flowing beneath them. I long for that. So I make it for myself here at night in my sitting room. A fire. And darkness but for it . . . I picture heaven as a garden, definitely. One that is perfect in climate and though you wander around so many souls, you don't have to be seen if you don't want to.

I do want to, though. Be seen. I've never been seen. Not even by me. I want to sing wherever I can get away with singing without upsetting God or my granny or my mother. I cause a lot of upset on this earth. Being the kind of person I am.

I've done only one holy thing in my life and that was sing. Only the business of music is so unholy. After a while they begin to clash. You just can't work right because you're in the wrong environment. Kind of like the acid not working in the rockabilly club. My spirit isn't suited for the business of music. Nor for anything, really. Other than making songs and performing them. Which is my love. Performing, I mean. Born for that. Yes, sir.

I wonder: In heaven, do they make songs? And whisper them to composers on earth? What am I saying. The Koran is like a song. And it was whispered to Gabriel and then by him to Muhammad. Took twenty-one years to complete. God's an incredible songwriter, actually.

I hope it's true God loves a singer. And I bet Muhammad must have had a beautiful voice. I hope he's still singing in nighttime paradise. Maybe if I just be quiet I'll hear him.

SEPTEMBER 25, 2019

I AM SO MOVED. People have been going nuts over my performance of "Nothing Compares 2 U" on Ireland's *Late Late Show*. It went viral. Two million people watched it online. And welcomed me home. To music.

All I have to do is not fuck it up. So far, so good; I've had only one little slip where I threatened the Irish State on Twitter. Then I told an obvious lie and said my Twitter account had been hacked and the tweet wasn't mine. Total lie. Crazy bitch.

But apart from that, I've done good. Three shows and no complaints; lots of crying men. That's how I know it's gone good—I get to make men cry for a good reason only when I sing. The rest of the time they're crying because I'm such a pain in the hole.

I wore a red abaya and matching hijab. Very Star Wars. Someone posted a picture of one of Emperor Palpatine's guards. Even I had to laugh. I gotta figure out some shorter hijabs. I like wearing them. I like my home in Islam. I like being identifiable by my brothers and sisters in the streets. I like representing. Because Islam gets a hard time. But I'm no soldier anymore. I only want to represent.

For shows, the hijab can be awkward because of the earpiece I'm using. I need to be able to fiddle with it during performances. I actually feel naked now if I don't wear something after a year of covering my hair. (In the summer, I didn't wear hijab because I couldn't handle the heat; I wore a light turban instead. I don't know how the ladies do it in the boiling-hot countries.)

I don't think anyone should be forced to wear hijab. But I don't think anyone should be forced *not* to wear it either. It should be a matter of choice. And in my case it is. To women who berate my choice and say I'm trying to conform to Eastern men's idea of beauty, I point out their bleached-blond hair is the same as a hijab—only theirs conforms to Western men's idea of beauty. And I suggest if they really don't like hijab they should shave their heads.

I'm not wearing it for beauty or for a man. I don't want to attract a man at my age. I'm as far from that as possible, although I wouldn't mind a companion if God has one in store who could put up with me or whom I could put up with. I wear what I love, that's all. But everything I wear to work is a statement. Otherwise my mother would slaughter me! The woman was a dressmaker and a model, and I'd feel her from heaven smiting me if I went onstage in my tracksuit and T-shirt.

As Yeats said, one cannot separate the dancer from the dance.

I'm totally shitting myself because my tour starts in three weeks and everyone expects me to be brilliant but I'm going to have only four days of rehearsals and it's been five years since I sang, so I'm frightened I won't be able to remember the words of sixteen songs. I'm so swamped in the house, I haven't had time to sit listening to the songs and my printer is fucked so I can't print them out. So I'm not going out to buy yet another damn printer. I'm cursed with the things; they die when I walk past them. And I'm agoraphobic as fuck. A thing I mention rarely.

Agoraphobia. I'm afraid in open spaces. Not of people. It's a PTSD thing. Home is safe. Hotels are safe. Work is safe. Inside the car is safe. What happens is I get into town and I panic; I need to be home. It's debilitating because it makes for a shit social life. Especially because I haven't actually told more than two of my friends about this problem. So people get mad at me because I make plans to go somewhere and always cancel. I mean to go when I make the plan, I want to go. But when it comes time to go, I panic and find a white lie for why I can't. I don't know why I lie. I guess I don't want people thinking I'm nuts.

POSTSCRIPT

MY MOST ESTEEMED FATHER,

I'm writing this little letter because I want you to either print it out and stick it on your mirror or have it tattooed on the inside of your lovely eyelids so you never doubt or blame yourself and/or my mother for my behavior or my mental-health conditions.

So here it is . . .

Sinéad, who happens by the utterly meaningless science of Allah to be your and Marie's beloved daughter, was *born*—through *zero* fault of yours *or* her mother's—with a set of brain abnormalities stemming from the O'Grady DNA that manifest in the form of mental illness.

Sinéad also suffered, at age eleven, an extremely serious head injury when a boy on a train going full speed through Blackrock Station opened a door outward and it hit her as she stood on the platform.

It has been scientifically proven that such head injuries can cause mental illness or make worse any mental illness a soul might have been born with.

Therefore, please know that your daughter would have been as nutty as a fuckin' fruitcake and as crazy as a loon even if she'd had Saint Joseph and the Virgin Mary for parents and grown up in the Little House on the Prairie.

Nothing in Sinéad's childhood environment or experience caused her mental illnesses. The evidence of this being *fact* is the rock-solid sanity of your and Marie's other three children.

Psychiatric and musical research has powerfully proven that all individuals upon whom Allah has chosen to breathe even the teeniest whisper of His musical fire are also by necessity endowed with insanity. And all musicians truly called by God are lunatics. Otherwise they'd be arrogant bastards. Humility is requirement number one of any artist truly called by God.

Also, all rock musicians are rule-breaking, delinquent, drug-guzzling pigs, careless sluts, unfit parents, and alcoholic maniacs—although not crazy enough for the nuthouse or criminal enough for the jail—whether they grew up in paradise or hell or anywhere in between.

That's why the music business was invented. Otherwise there'd have been nowhere to house the likes of Little Richard and Liberace. 😊

So, she was born bonkers.

Neither you nor her mother are responsible. You both did your very best with the tools God had given you. And your daughter remembers only everything wonderful you both gave her. Most important in your case, songs, singing, and Allah.

So don't be kicking the walls unless it's just for fun.

And always remember that Allah has you and your children in His mouth, like a lioness carries her cubs. And that trouble is only God in disguise.

And there's a throne in heaven for you, encrusted with a jewel for every white hair your wild child ever gave you.

Sinéad/Shuhada

EPILOGUE

TODAY IS APRIL 5, 2020. The world is on lockdown. No one knows when or in what form life will "return to normal." As if it ever was before.

The way we've been living, maybe it will change. We might continue to love each other as much as we currently are by staying home. You just never know. But there's gonna be a journey through seven hells. I can somewhat help some loved ones negotiate this, having had plenty of training in such travels. When one lives with the devil, one finds out there's a God.

In America, Trump wants everyone to go back to work, right at the crest of the virus's wave. And he wants sick people to take some drug he knows nothing about, but he won't wear a mask. He's the king of Kool-Aid. He says he can't be meeting presidents, dictators, kings, or queens while wearing a mask. And only last week some princess of Europe died, actually. Of the virus.

The people are to blame. If Trump were an Irish president or prime minister, he'd have been physically ripped out of office the day he first gave away someone's child at any border. He's mentally ill. The so-called sane people are at best doing nothing and at worst enabling him. Like some giant emperor who has no clothes. Which is all he is. A lesson for the people not to be so fuckin' nice all the time. I mean, none of the reporters ever ask him, "Sir, what is wrong with you?" Negligence. The desire to be polite, it's killing them. And it goes on and on. No matter what he does.

Time was, Americans went out into the streets to peacefully fight for each other's civil rights. Now none of them can even go out.

What will they do with this monster when they can? History has cleverly made *socialism* the worst word one can utter in America. Perhaps, though, a terrible beauty might be born.

I'm sitting outside on my porch steps facing the sea. I smoke too much to be indoors. I'm examining my life and how I want it to be when this is all over. I'm aware it's gonna go on a long time. The lockdown, I mean. And acutely aware I have very little control of how I live my life, certainly for the next year. Because my shows that were canceled due to the virus have to be performed in early 2021. I can't shift them to that summer. Unless a miracle happens. See, I want to go to college. It's a one-year course in health-care assistance. Starts every September in my local vocational school. Finishes June. But something always gets in the way. I tried to go two years ago but I was not well enough. Last year I needed to work, to perform, because after not being well for four years, I came out of the hospital in May with eight grand in the bank and promptly got a two-grand heating bill for my house, which had stood empty and neglected while I was gone.

I was hoping I could tour this September. Because if I had gone two years ago, I'd be on the front lines now, helping people. The government has asked for health-care assistants to pitch in. As it is, as I said, I'm sitting on my ass doing nothing but gaining weight. So I've decided to start school in autumn 2020 and go out on tour again (I hope) in the summer of 2021. I've made my mind up to do it and put the money aside for it now while I have it. Then, between albums and tours, I'll have an occupation. Not be sitting round for a year at a time with nothing but idle hands.

Because of the virus, it feels like the end of the world and the beginning of another.

Maybe a better one.

BP FALLON